Praying with the Saints for

THE + HOLY + SOULS
in PURGATORY

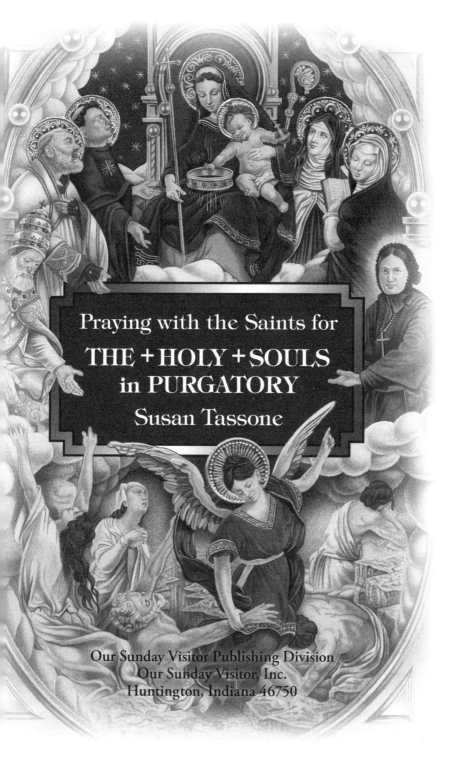

Praying with the Saints for

THE + HOLY + SOULS
in PURGATORY

Susan Tassone

Our Sunday Visitor Publishing Division
Our Sunday Visitor, Inc.
Huntington, Indiana 46750

Nihil Obstat
Reverend Michael Heintz, Ph.D.
Censor Librorum

Imprimatur
✠ John M. D'Arcy
Bishop of Fort Wayne-South Bend
June 24, 2009

The *Nihil Obstat* and *Imprimatur* are official declarations that a book is free from doctrinal or moral error. It is not implied that those who have granted the *Nihil Obstat* and *Imprimatur* agree with the contents, opinions, or statements expressed.

ISBN: 978-1-59276-551-5 (Inventory No. T833)
LCCN: 2009932451

Cover design: Amanda Miller
Cover art: Jed Gibbons
Interior design: Sherri L. Hoffman
Interior art: Jed Gibbons

PRINTED IN THE UNITED STATES OF AMERICA

*Dedicated to the most grateful souls,
especially my ancestors.
Rest in peace!*

Of Prayer, of Love, and of Contact with Other Worlds

... Be not forgetful of prayer. Every time you pray, if your prayer is sincere, there will be new feeling and new meaning in it, which will give you fresh courage, and you will understand that prayer is an education.

Remember, too, every day, and whenever you can, repeat to yourself, *"Lord, have mercy on all who appear before Thee today."* For every hour and every moment thousands of men leave life on this earth, and their souls appear before God. And how many of them depart in solitude, unknown, sad, dejected that no one mourns for them or even knows whether they have lived or not!

And behold, from the other end of the earth perhaps, your prayer for their rest will rise up to God though you knew them not nor they you. How touching it must be to a soul standing in dread before the Lord to feel at that instant that, for him too, there is one to pray, that there is a fellow creature left on earth to love him too!

And God will look on you both more graciously, for if you have had so much pity on him, how much will He have pity Who is infinitely more loving and merciful than you. And He will forgive him for your sake.

FATHER ZOSIMA,
IN DOSTOYEVSKY'S *THE BROTHERS KARAMAZOV*

TABLE OF CONTENTS

PREFACE

All down the centuries, the Catholic Church, true to her belief in the Communion of Saints which she professes in the Apostles' Creed, has urged the faithful to pray fervently for the souls of their deceased brethren in purgatory. They are often called "poor souls" because they cannot help themselves, depending fully on our prayers to be able to cleanse themselves of the residue of their sinful past and enter into God's beatific presence to become our grateful intercessors before his heavenly throne. Among these we must mention those who have been long forgotten by their relatives and friends on earth: we call them the "abandoned souls in purgatory."

Over the years, Susan Tassone has been tirelessly writing and teaching about this revered tradition of praying for the holy souls in purgatory. Her meticulous research and attention to both historical and spiritual detail has helped many to understand more deeply the value of this singular devotion and selfless way of prayer. In her latest book, *Praying with the Saints for the Holy Souls in Purgatory*, she has brought a whole new dimension to this devotion, seeing it through the spiritual writings and tradition of saints throughout the centuries. The book presents the writings and spiritual legacy of saints from all corners of the world and through all ages, thus demonstrating the universal interest in praying, with and through the saints, for the holy souls.

Susan's singular crusade has led her compassionate heart to add a missionary dimension to her special ministry, a dimension that envisages using the devotion to give tangible support to priests in areas where the faithful are unfamiliar with or unable to offer Mass intentions in support of their pastors. This ministry consists of collecting Mass intentions, or stipends, for the poor souls in purgatory, and then allocating these funds for the needs of priests toiling hard in the missions throughout the world. The generosity of so many who have been deeply touched by this ministry in favor of the holy souls has thus provided a new means of sustenance to many priests in mission territories. Among these are retired diocesan and religious priests, seminary professors, members of missionary monastic communities, and priests living in remote difficult areas and poor village parishes lost in some faraway forest or jungle.

Thanks to these untiring efforts, assistance has gone out through cardinals, apostolic nuncios, archbishops, and bishops to help support diocesan and missionary clergy who gratefully fulfill the obligations of offering Masses for the poor souls, and who also invoke God's special blessings and protection on the donors of the Mass stipends.

In combining the devotion to the holy souls with support for mission personnel, Susan sets a wonderful example of lay collaboration in the Church's evangelizing mission. For it encourages a lay participation in missionary endeavors that goes beyond territorial borders and cultures, and which also brings together men and women of all parts of the world in a chorus of praise, prayer, and thanksgiving for the salvation of those who have "gone before us marked with the sign of faith" (Eucharistic Prayer I).

It is a distinct privilege for me to present Susan Tassone's latest work on the writings and devotion of saints throughout the ages to the souls in purgatory. I would like to add a special word of thanks on behalf of the missions throughout the world, because she has given her very laudable ministry a powerful missionary thrust. May the chapters and practical suggestions for daily and seasonal prayers made in this book lead to an ever wider and deeper appreciation of the precious devotion to the holy souls in purgatory.

✠ Ivan Cardinal Dias
Prefect of the Congregation
for the Evangelization of Peoples

INTRODUCTION

*"My beloved dead, I remember you and love you always.
Pray for me."*

— Blessed John XXIII

My Personal Pilgrimage

How did I get involved with the holy souls in purgatory?

I want to share why I got involved and tell a little bit about how God is working in my life to help you understand what I experienced. On August 11, 1983, the feast of my patron, St. Susanna, I was hit head on and injured by a cab, which left my left leg damaged. My doctor told me that my leg was permanently damaged, and that I would have constant bouts of painful swelling and tenderness of the leg for the rest of my life.

The date was even more significant. Fifty years earlier, on that very same day, my great aunt, known as "Little Mary," who was ten years old at the time, was also injured in a car accident. She died. I survived. A priest told me that my life was spared and that I had a mission. He said that sometimes a sacrifice is made in the family for a greater cause. It shook me up.

I have had a special bond with the Blessed Mother since I was a child. My mother was very active in the parish, and we were very young when she planted the seed for the love of Our Lady in our hearts. (I remember, for example, we had the Pilgrim Virgin statue in our home.)

In 1993, with the permission of my doctor, I decided to go on pilgrimage to a Marian shrine, to pay a visit to my best friend, Our Lady. I did not go for a cure. That never occurred to me! I expected to pray, to experience closeness with Our Lady, and to return home. Our Blessed Mother had other plans. My leg, my permanently damaged leg, was healed. My doctor said it was a miracle and that I was blessed. However, he waited three years before he would document the healing. He wanted to be sure it was real. Three years later I delivered a letter from the doctor to the shrine. It is one of the documented medical cases of registered healings.

When I returned home, I realized Our Lady had other surprises for me. Someone gave me a booklet called *Read Me or Rue It*. It was about the plight of the holy souls in purgatory. I was fascinated with the stories about the holy souls and how they intercede for those who relieve their sufferings. These souls were in desperate need of our Masses.

The booklet said the holy souls would repay you 10,000 times. I liked the idea. I needed all the friends I could get! It was like quid pro quo: You help me, and I will help you. I wanted all my family and friends to reach God. I identified with the holy souls. I don't like being cooped up. I am a free spirit. I like my freedom. Why not help release them so they can reach heaven? Free them!

I took it upon myself to become a missionary for our holy heroes. In my journey, I began to understand how critical the doctrine of purgatory is to our faith, how purgatory is a very positive and consoling part of that faith.

I began collecting Mass stipends for the holy souls in purgatory. People of every faith gave donations. I soon realized that they were hungry for God. I collected $763 and brought the donation to my pastor. To my surprise, he was unable to accept the donation because he was the only priest in the parish and his Mass-intentions book was filled. For the first time, it personally struck home how we need to pray for vocations to the priesthood. The priest sent me to the Catholic Missions Office — or, as it's officially called, the Propagation of the Faith. Every diocese has one. Its purpose is to support our missionary priests all over the world through our prayers and donations.

By virtue of our baptism, we are called by name to participate in the saving mission of Jesus Christ. We are called to share in the responsibility to witness to God's unconditional love and to bring the healing presence of Christ to our world.

The pastor told me the Missions Office was in dire need of Mass stipends. These offerings support the priests' ministry and the life of the Church. "The Christian faithful who give an offering to apply the Mass for their intention contribute to the good of the Church and by that offering share its concern to support its ministers and works" (*Code of Canon Law*, 946).

Over the years, Mass stipend donations had greatly diminished. This would seem to point to two attitudes: the forgetfulness of prayer and the impression that the Church is able to fulfill its role without the necessary resources. My pastor had just received a letter from the Missions Office begging for Mass stipends. How providential that I would approach him at that time.

I visited the Missions Director and learned again how desperately our Catholic missionary priests needed Mass stipends. Many times those gifts are their sole income because the people of the countries where they serve are too poor to donate financially. When a priest witnesses a wedding, baptizes an infant, or buries a parishioner who has died, the people are unable to make a monetary offering and, instead, may give him a chicken or some items from their harvest.

I learned, too, that many people around the world only attend Mass once a year because the priest has no stipends to even purchase bread and wine for the Eucharist. He has no money to buy gas to put in the jeep to reach remote locales to celebrate Mass. Many times, Mass stipends buy books for seminarians. The Mission Director asked me what you get when you buy books for seminarians. Then she answered the question herself: You get a priest for forty years! That did it for me. I wanted to help.

Since 1993, I have waged a crusade for the holy souls in purgatory collecting Mass stipends — anything I could do for our missionaries and suffering friends in need. I tried to promote this through television, radio, Internet, print media, public speaking, and writing. To date, more than two million dollars has been raised for Mass stipends for our missionary priests because of readers like you. I like to see it as two million souls released from purgatory.

This work has been an extraordinary grace for me. It has become my mission. The fruits of this ministry are obvious: a greater appreciation and support for our missionaries around the world, praying more with the heart, a keener insight into the plight of the holy souls and more awareness of their pain, and an increase of love of God and neighbor — both those living and those deceased.

I invite you to join me and answer the call in one of the most solid and noble devotions of our Catholic faith. This is a tremendous act of supernatural charity. It unites souls to God and assists our missionary priests and mission orders who are helping people of all ages in some of the poorest segments of our world through their evangelizing, catechizing, preaching, celebrating the Mass, and administering of the sacraments.

We often feel that we do nothing for the Lord; that our love is weak, our lives are poor in good works, and our progress in virtue is almost invisible. Here, then, is a way of doing something for Jesus which we know will delight him: namely, helping to release the suffering souls by the Eucharist and other suffrages (prayers, indulgences, works of penance, almsgiving), and so swell the ranks of the glorified in heaven.

The holy souls will not forget those who opened their prison gates. They think more of us than we do of them. They are more solicitous for our salvation than they were for their own while they were on earth. The holy souls want us to work while it is still day. They beg us to make good use of our time and to perform the work and mission that has been given to us by God. They render unto us a thousandfold for our prayers, obtaining for us help and graces of which we have never dreamed of asking as they push us — almost in spite of ourselves — along the road to heaven.

My journey has deepened my faith tremendously, allowing me to better see the goodness and mercy of God, and to join with my fellow supplicants in celebrating the beauty of our faith.

My heartfelt thanks to: Michael Brown, of SpiritDaily.com, who encouraged me to write about the saints and souls. This book would not have been born if it were not for him. To Jackie Lindsey (my acquisitions editor), project editor George Foster, and the OSV staff, who walk the talk on purgatory. To Steven Jay Gross, my friend, confidant, coach. Thank you will never be adequate in this life. To Michael Wick, Executive Director, Institute on Religious Life. He is a creative genius for the Lord. To Ann Maksymiec, who keeps impeccable records. To librarians Anna Kielian at the University of St. Mary of the Lake/Mundelein Seminary, Mundelein, Illinois, and Vanessa Crouther at Loyola University Chicago. Their assistance over the years has been outstanding. To Father Joe McCabe, M.M., missionary priest par excellence. Father Joe gave me the privilege of a lifetime when I met with the Roman Curia and apostolic nuncios, from whom I heard firsthand the plight of missionary priests and their gratitude for our assistance.

And to Our Lady, my life, my sweetness, and all my hope.

PART I
What Do We Know About Purgatory and the Holy Souls?

"As we enter heaven, we will see them, so many of them, coming towards us and thanking us. We will ask who they are and they will say: 'A poor soul you prayed for in purgatory!'"

— ARCHBISHOP FULTON J. SHEEN

What is purgatory? Where is it located? Why does purgatory exist? Who are the holy souls? What do they suffer? Can we pray for the holy souls? Can they pray for us? Can we avoid purgatory?

In this section, we will answers those questions — and more — in light of the Church's teachings and our rich Catholic tradition so that we may grow in love and devotion, and fulfill our charitable obligation to the souls in purgatory.

What Is Purgatory?

It was a holy and wholesome thought to pray for the dead, that they may be loosed from their sins.
— 2 MACCABEES 12:45 (DOUAY-RHEIMS)

This thought is appropriately called holy because it springs from a holy source, that of faith and charity. It is called wholesome first to the poor souls themselves because it comforts and encourages them in their sufferings. And for those who pray for them, it increases their own merits and gains new, faithful friends in heaven.

As the *Catechism of the Catholic Church* (CCC) (1030-1031) teaches:

All who die in God's grace and friendship, but still imperfectly purified, are indeed assured of their eternal salvation; but after death they undergo purification, so as to achieve the holiness necessary to enter the joy of heaven.

The Church gives the name *Purgatory* [from the Latin *purgare*, meaning to make clean or purify] to this final purification of the elect, which is entirely different from the punishment of the damned. The Church formulated her doctrine of faith on Purgatory especially at the Councils of Florence and Trent....

This teaching is also based on the practice of prayer for the dead, already mentioned in Sacred Scripture: "Therefore, [Judas Maccabeus] made atonement for the dead that they might be delivered from their sin" (2 Mac 12:45).

Prayer for the deceased clearly implies that there is a purgatory of some kind. The Scriptures speak of a cleansing fire after death (1 Cor 3:15 and 1 Pt 1:7; see also Mt 12:32). In fact, it was not until the sixteenth-century Protestant revolt against the Church that any significant opposition to prayers for the dead occurred.

A more personal definition of purgatory came from my then ten-year-old godchild. She told my mother, "Grandma, Aunt Susie said there are only three places you can go." Grandma concurred. Angela continued, "Heaven, hell, and *puberty!*" Out of the mouths of babes. For some of us puberty is worse than purgatory! Angela was correct, though. Purgatory is a training ground, or as the poet Dante put it: "It is the place where human spirits purge themselves, and train to leap up into joy celestial" (Dante, *Purgatory* I. 5-6).

Where Is Purgatory Located?

By the waters of Babylon, where we sat down and wept, when we remembered Zion.

— PSALM 137:1

In his general audience on August 4, 1999, Pope John Paul II stressed that the term "purgatory" does not indicate a place, but rather "a condition of existence" of "those who, after death, exist in a state of purification." He said, "Every trace of attachment to evil must be eliminated, every imperfection of the soul corrected. Purification must be complete, and indeed this is precisely what is meant by the Church's teaching on *purgatory.*"

Why Does Purgatory Exist?

Nothing unclean shall enter it.
— Revelation 21:27

The Church is clear that purgatory exists as a gracious gift of God's love, a masterpiece of his supreme mercy. God loves us more than anybody else and more than anybody can. He burns for love of us and his love is likened to fire: "The Lord your God is a devouring fire" (Dt 4:24). Purgatory exists because of God's love and his incomprehensible holiness. It's his love that cleanses and purifies us to be able to stand before his presence. Because of our sin and selfishness we need purification and healing. This is a loving purgatory, not a purgatory of punishment.

God is a God of unspeakable purity. The very vision of God causes eternal purity and blessedness. It is the sublime beauty of God that ravishes these souls, and they will not go before him with the least stain. The souls willingly flee into the cleansing of purification so they are able to see God. Purgatory is a place of great restoration; a place where our imperfections and faults are purified to reflect the radiant image of God.

Several years ago, Cardinal Joseph Ratzinger (now Pope Benedict XVI) eloquently put it this way:

> I would go so far as to say that if there was no purgatory, then we would have to invent it, for who would dare say of himself that he was able to stand directly before God? And yet we don't want to be, to use an image from Scripture, "a pot that turned out wrong," that has to be thrown away; we want to be able to be put right. Purgatory basically means that God can put the pieces back together again. That he can cleanse us in such a way that we are able to be with him and can stand there in the fullness of life....
>
> [Purgatory] strips off from one person what is unbearable and from another the inability to bear certain things,

so that in each of them a pure heart is revealed, and we can see that we all belong together in one enormous symphony of being. (*God and the World*, p. 130)

Who Are the Holy Souls?

"Charity is incomplete until it includes the dead as well as the living."

— ST. THOMAS AQUINAS

The souls in purgatory are those who died in the state of grace but who are not yet cleansed from sin to enter heaven. The holy souls are linked to us by faith.

As part of the Mystical Body of Christ, the souls in purgatory are called the "Church Suffering," those who are expiating their sins in purgatory. Our lot as children of the "Church Militant," those of us who are still pilgrims on earth, includes not only being able to gain merit for ourselves but also to provide for the dead and give part of our satisfactions to our brothers and sisters of the "Church Suffering" in purgatory.

When their time of purification is complete, they join the holy ranks of the angels and saints as part of the "Church Triumphant," the faithful who have already reached their heavenly home. The angels and saints help the souls in purgatory not by way of merit or satisfaction but by their prayers and intercession with God.

As believers we see the Church as the family of God. Who is part of our family? Those who shared our joys and sorrows: our mothers, fathers, children, grandparents, grandchildren, brothers, sisters, aunts, uncles, cousins, nieces, and nephews. And those who took a special interest in us: godparents, friends, teachers, neighbors, religious, and benefactors. All those who have been entwined into the fabric of our lives, will in death, be part of us through our prayers and suffrages.

In an exclusive interview in 1985 on the state of the Church, Cardinal Joseph Ratzinger, then Prefect of the Sacred Congregation for the Doctrine of the Faith, reflected: "Praying for one's departed loved ones is a far too immediate urge to be suppressed; it is a most beautiful manifestation of solidarity, love and assistance, reaching beyond the barrier of death. The happiness or unhappiness of a person dear to me, who has now crossed to the other shore, depends in part on whether I remember or forget him; he does not stop needing my love" (*The Ratzinger Report*, pp. 146-147).

What Do the Holy Souls Suffer?

My soul thirsts for thee like a parched land.
— PSALM 143:6

Purgatory is *not* the inferno we may have imagined as a child where souls are surrounded by flames of fire! Their suffering is one of longing and unease from their separation from God. They see him and know him, but are not fully united with him.

No sooner has the soul departed this life than it beholds God, and from this "sight" the soul receives at once so deep and vivid a knowledge of God and all his infinite perfections that it is utterly incapable of being occupied with anything other than the divine beauty and goodness.

The soul feels so drawn toward God that it finds it impossible to wish, to seek, to love anything but God. The soul experiences at once an insatiable hunger and thirst after God. It feels an indescribable love for God, and it "burns" for this love. The holy souls burn with a "spiritual fever," a yearning for God which surpasses the heat of any earthly fire. So we rightly speak of the "fire" of purgatory and of the cleansing flames of love with which Divine Charity reaches out to purify the holy souls.

In his 2007 encyclical *Spe Salvi*, ("Saved in Hope"), Pope Benedict XVI wonderfully captures the essence of the purifying nature of this Divine Love:

Some recent theologians are of the opinion that the fire which both burns and saves is Christ himself, the Judge, and Savior. The encounter with him is the decisive act of judgment. Before his gaze all falsehood melts away. This encounter with him, as it burns us, transforms and frees us, allowing us to become truly ourselves. All that we build during our lives can prove to be mere straw, pure bluster, and it collapses. Yet in the pain of this encounter, when the impurity and sickness of our lives become evident to us, there lies salvation. His gaze, the touch of his heart heals us through an undeniably painful transformation "as through fire." But it is a blessed pain, in which the holy power of his love sears through us like a flame, enabling us to become totally ourselves and thus totally of God. (n. 47)

A departed soul once told St. Margaret Mary Alacoque that willingly would they suffer until Judgment Day if only they could see Jesus gazing on them with love. They want to give him unceasing glory. They want to contemplate him, possess him, and praise him forever in unison with the angels. Even the damned are tortured by this same desire.

We are made for God alone. God created us for this. St. Augustine exclaims: "You have created us for yourself, O Lord, and our hearts are restless until they rest in you."

We often hear, "Oh, the soul of this or that person is certainly in heaven," and so we fail to pray for him or her. How often does this false charity cause souls to suffer and delay their entry into heaven? Only God knows the state of a soul at death. Let us rather be advocates by our prayers and turn that pain into everlasting joy.

Why Do We Pray for the Holy Souls?

"You the living can do everything for us, and we can do everything for you. It is an exchange of prayers."

— A Holy Soul

As faithful Jews, Jesus and the apostles joined in prayers for the deceased. St. Clement stated that St. Peter liked to have prayers said for the relief of those who had passed away.

St. Paul implies the existence of purgatory in his prayer for Onesiphorus: "May the Lord grant him to find mercy from the Lord on that Day" (2 Tim 1:18). This is equivalent to the invocation to the Lord to "grant eternal rest" to the faithful departed.

Around 190, a document called *The Passion of Perpetua and Felicity,* martyrs of the early Church, described St. Perpetua's vision regarding her deceased brother who was in pain. She "prayed for him night and day," wailing and crying that her prayers be granted. Several days later, in another vision, Perpetua learned of the end of his pain and of his peace with God.

From the earliest days, the inscriptions in the catacombs of Rome and elsewhere testify to prayer for the dead with words of petition for peace and rest.

The third-century theologian Tertullian tells us the faithful prayed at the tombs to make intercession for their departed: "We offer sacrifices for the dead on their birthday anniversaries" and on the anniversaries of their deaths.

The Church Fathers (renowned figures of the early Church) speak the same words of faith and conviction regarding purgatory and make the same moving appeal on behalf of the holy souls in purgatory.

St. Ephrem (d. 373) stressed the value of prayers for the dead: "Instead of shedding useless tears over the grave let them flow at prayers in church, for in these there is help and comfort for the dead as well as for the living."

St. Cyril of Jerusalem (d. 386) expressed the following:

Then we make mention also of those who have already fallen asleep: first, the patriarchs, prophets, apostles, and martyrs, that through their prayers and supplications God would receive our petition; next, we make mention also of the holy fathers and bishops who have already fallen asleep, and, to put it simply, of all among us who have already fallen asleep, for we believe that it will be of very great benefit to the souls of those for whom the petition is carried up, while this holy and most solemn sacrifice is laid out.

St. Ambrose (d. 397) offered a touching prayer in the funeral sermon he gave for the Roman Emperor Theodosius:

Grant, O Lord, to thy servant Emperor Theodosius that rest which Thou has prepared for thy saints. May his soul soar up to where it came, where it can no more feel the sting of death, and where it will learn that death is not the end of life, but of sin. I loved him, and therefore, I will follow him in the land of the living; I will not leave him until by my prayers and lamentations he will be admitted unto the holy mount of the Lord.

Our charity and gratitude not only demand that we pray for the souls in purgatory, but our faith requires our prayers to help them join the House of the Lord. Very few of us have souls free from defects, but through our prayers and sacrifices we can create a soul without blemish.

God's justice demands expiation for sin. Christ told St. Faustina, a great Polish messenger of Divine Mercy, "All these souls are greatly loved by Me. They are making retribution to My justice. It is in your power to bring relief. Draw all the indulgences from the treasury of My Church and offer them on their behalf. Oh, if you only knew the torments they suffer.... My mercy does not want this, but justice demands it" (*Diary,* 1226, 20).

God has given us the power and privilege to relieve and assist the holy souls and hasten their uniting with him. He places in our hands all the means necessary to help them reach heaven. Unless these holy ones are released by the good works of the faithful,

God in his ineffable justice is resolved to purify them in purgatory. It is also a duty of personal interest since one day we may expect others to help us in the same way.

Souls must undergo purification necessary for heaven, and they beg for our prayers, suffrages, and good works. Their time of personal merit is up. They can do nothing — nothing — for their deliverance. These suffering friends of God cannot do penance. They cannot gain indulgences. They cannot receive the sacraments. They cannot perform new meritorious acts. *They depend entirely on our charity.* Are we listening?

We are invited to join with the Church on behalf of the Church Suffering through our intercessory prayer and the power of this kind of prayer. Since Abraham, intercession (asking on behalf of one another) has been characteristic of a heart attuned to God's mercy.

If Purgatory Is Simply Purification, How Can a Third Party Intervene?

Whoever brings back a sinner from the error of his way will save his soul from death and will cover a multitude of sins.
— James 5:20

Pope Benedict XVI addresses intercessory prayer and defends prayers for the dead like this:

No man is an island, entire of itself. Our lives are involved with one another, through innumerable interactions they are linked together. No one lives alone. No one sins alone. No one is saved alone. The lives of others continually spill over into mine in what I think, say, do and achieve. And conversely, my life spills over into that of others: for better and for worse. So my prayer for another is not something extraneous to that person, something external, not even after death. In the interconnectedness of Being, my gratitude to the other — my prayer for him — can play a certain part in his purification. (*Spe Salvi*, n. 48)

The power of intercessory prayer in offering sacrifices for the dead augments our merit in the sight of God, earns mercy for us if we are in purgatory, multiplies intercessors for us who are still crusading on earth, and ultimately swells the Church Triumphant.

Prayer, Sister Agnes, and Mr. Morrison: A True Story

"Repentance opens heaven."
— ST. JOHN CHRYSOSTOM

"I'm dying, Sister," Mr. Morrison said in a low, gruff voice. "I don't know what you could do to help me."

Sister Agnes looked at the old man sitting up in bed and somehow his face was familiar! "Well, I really would like to pray for you," she answered. "It's never too late to say a prayer."

As their conversation progressed, Mr. Morrison admitted, "I don't know if God wants to hear about me. I've done a lot of bad things in my life."

"No matter what you have done," the nun assured him, "God will forgive you. You just need to ask him with a sincere heart. And after you've died, I'll continue to pray for you."

The idea of prayers for the dead startled him. "After I've died? Why would you pray for me after I'm dead? What good is that?"

"There's always hope!" Sister Agnes insisted. "Are you Catholic?"

"No," the man said, "I never really spent much time in any church."

Sister Agnes explained, "Catholics believe that if you ask God to forgive your sins before you die, you'll eventually get to heaven. And we believe that by praying for people we can help them even after they have died. It's from the Old Testament."

The man said nothing more and, after he had gently closed his eyes, Sister Agnes quietly left his room.

When Sister Agnes returned a few days later, Mr. Morrison's face seemed even paler than before, and he labored for every breath. Even so, he struggled to sit up in bed as soon as she entered the room. "One of the nurses said you wanted to see me," the nun said.

"I'd like to know more about what it means to be a Catholic," the man responded.

Sister Agnes smiled. "What did I say the other day that interested you?" she asked.

"Sister," he began, "for longer than I can remember, the people around me have only seemed to care about how much money they could make off me. Now you're telling me that people will care enough about me to pray for me even after I'm gone! I like the sound of that!"

In the days that followed, Sister Agnes met with the man regularly to teach him all that she could about the Catholic faith. After that, Mr. Morrison was baptized.

A few weeks later, in early June 1979, Mr. Morrison died. Hundreds came to mourn his passing. They remembered what a famous actor he was. But Sister Agnes could only remember how appreciative Marion Morrison (also known as John Wayne) had been. How grateful he had been to know that someone cared enough to pray for him, both now and in the days to come.

So it is with the "Church Suffering" that we act as "intercessors."

What Is the Origin of All Souls Day on November 2?

"As one whom his mother comforts, so I will comfort you."
— ISAIAH 66:13

This feast commemorating all the faithful departed souls in purgatory was instituted in the Benedictine Monastery of Cluny, France, by Abbot Odilo in 998. St. Odilo was always very devoted to the holy souls and offered all his prayers, sufferings, and mortifications for their release from purgatory.

A French pilgrim, when coming back from Jerusalem, happened to meet a pious hermit who told him that he often heard the cries of the souls in purgatory but they were soon discharged because of the suffrages of the faithful and in particular the devout prayers of the monks of Cluny. He also heard the voices of evil spirits shouting against Abbot Odilo.

When the abbot learned this, he praised God for his mercy in hearing the innocent prayers of his monks. St. Odilo directed that all the monks observe a special day of commemoration for the holy souls on November 2, after the feast of All Saints. It was accepted in Rome in the fourteenth century. In 1915 Pope Benedict XV issued an apostolic constitution that granted all priests the privilege of celebrating three Masses on that day for the following intentions: one for the faithful departed, one for a particular intention, and one for the intention of the pope.

The whole month of November is dedicated to the holy souls in purgatory (while most of the saints only have one feast day in their honor). That tradition has its roots in ancient Mosaic Law. Among the Israelites, the "month of the dead" was one of the most general and customary forms of devotion for the deceased. Certainly, prayer on behalf of the dead appears to be one of their most notable rites.

For example, Jacob was mourned for a total of seventy days: "So the physicians embalmed [Jacob]; forty days were required for it.... And the Egyptians wept for him seventy days." It was the same on the death of the high priest, Aaron; and of his brother, Moses (Dt 34:8). The people of Israel believed that there was no better way they could show their gratitude to these great men than by offering supplications to God.

This pious practice of praying for the departed during an entire uninterrupted month became so deeply rooted among the chosen people that Scripture tells us mourning is only complete when the deceased has been remembered and mourned during thirty days.

What Is the Best Way We Can Help the Holy Souls Reach Heaven?

"O Holy Host, you that break down the gates of Purgatory and open the door of the Kingdom of Heaven to the Faithful!"
— St. Peter Damian

Imagine a beneficent king leaves his guilty friend in prison for justice's sake. He waits with longing for one of his nobles to plead for the prisoner and offer something for the man's release and then he joyfully sets the prisoner free. Similarly, Our Lord accepts with highest pleasure what is offered to him for the poor souls because he longs inexpressibly to have near him those for whom he suffered so great a price.

There are a number of things we know about speaking to that "beneficent king," about our God and our prayers:

- Prayer is crucial in our lives.
- Through it, we raise our hearts and minds to God in praise and thanksgiving.
- God wants us to pray.
- It is in prayer that we meet him.
- Prayer is our vital and personal relationship with the true and living God.
- Prayer works miracles.
- We are bound to pray during this life if we wish to enjoy the bliss of heaven.
- Prayer is the key to heaven. It is an indispensable means of attaining salvation for ourselves and our deceased loved ones.
- Fervent, submissive prayer penetrates the clouds and moves God's heart to mercy.
- Through prayer, we are made holy, and this contributes to the holiness of the Church itself which is the Communion of Saints.

We also know this: The Holy Mass is the highest act of worship and the highest form of prayer. Or, in the words of St. Cyril: "We pray for all who have departed in this life, with the most confident conviction that the prayers at the altar are the most profitable to them."

When writing about the Mass and the relationship between the living and the dead, St. Augustine (d. 430) called it "the sacrament of love, the revelation of unity, and the bond of friendship." His prayer for his mother, St. Monica, is another important testimony from the early Church about supplications for the dead. He wrote:

> Forgive her, O Lord, forgive her, I beseech thee; "enter not into judgment" (Ps 143:2) with her. Let thy mercy be exalted above thy justice, for thy words are true and thou hast promised mercy to the merciful, that the merciful shall obtain mercy (Mt 5:7). (*Confessions*, 9, 13, 35)

St. Monica is quoted by her saintly son as telling him at the end of her life to "Lay this body anywhere, and do not let the care of it be a trouble to you at all." She goes on to say, "Only this I ask: that you will remember me at the Lord's altar, wherever you are" (*Confessions*, 9, 11, 27).

Some eight centuries later, while celebrating Mass in a church near the Three Fountains of St. Paul in Rome, St. Bernard of Clairvaux (d. 1153) saw a ladder stretching from earth to heaven with angels descending and ascending on it. They took souls from purgatory and led them into paradise. A painting depicting this hangs over the same altar where he offered Masses for the suffering souls.

And in our own time, the *Catechism of the Catholic Church* teaches: "From the beginning the Church has honored the memory of the dead by offering prayers in suffrage for them, above all the Eucharistic sacrifice, so that, thus purified, they may attain the beatific vision of God" (1032).

Even more recently, in his apostolic exhortation *Sacramentum Caritatis* (Sacrament of Charity), Pope Benedict XVI writes:

> The Eucharistic celebration, in which we proclaim that Christ has died and risen, and will come again, is a pledge of the future glory in which our bodies, too, will be glorified. Celebrating the memorial of our salvation strengthens our hope in the resurrection of the body and in the possibility of meeting once again, face to face, those who have gone before us marked with the sign of faith. In this context, I wish together with the Synod Fathers, to remind all the faithful of the importance of prayers for the dead, especially the offering of Mass for them, so that once purified, they can come to the beatific vision of God. A rediscovery of the eschatological dimension inherent in the Eucharist, celebrated and adored, will help sustain us on our journey and comfort us in the hope of glory (cf. Rom 5:2; Titus 2:13).

The gift we offer is not an earthly crown, but is the body and blood of God's own well-beloved Son, who has bled for the sins of the whole world. The Holy Sacrifice of the Mass is the most effective and powerful means we have to relieve the suffering souls in purgatory and deliver them from it.

The Church also commends indulgences (the remission of the debt of temporal punishment due to sin after its guilt is forgiven) and works of penance to be undertaken on behalf of the dead. (The Church's teaching on indulgences will be explained more in Part II.)

Since the Eucharist Is a Pledge of Our Future Glory, How Can Mass Be Medicine for Unforgiven Souls?

"The Holy Eucharist is my interior rule, my source of love, my inspiration in life."

— St. Peter Julian Eymard

The Eucharist not only purifies the souls of those who have died but also heals the living as they come into deeper relationship with Jesus. "For apologies that are hard to accept and people that are hard to forgive, the Mass is the key to opening our souls to reconciliation, says Benedict XVI" (Zenit.org, September 21, 2008). In his homily at the Cathedral of Albano, the Holy Father continued:

> The altar of sacrifice becomes in a certain way the point of encounter between heaven and earth.... Every time that you come to the altar for the Eucharistic celebration your soul opens to forgiveness and fraternal reconciliation, ready to accept the apologies of those who have hurt you and ready, in turn, to forgive.

Are My Prayers Wasted If the Soul Is Already in Heaven?

Pray constantly.
— 1 THESSALONIANS 5:17

No prayer is ever wasted with God. If deceased persons are prayed for by offering the Eucharist or by any prayer and have no further need of purification, the prayers are not unavailing. The deceased in heaven receives an increase in their intimacy of God's love and an increase in their own intercessory power as "we are surrounded by so great a cloud of witnesses" (Heb 12:1). St. Thomas Aquinas called this "accidental glory." God is never outdone in generosity!

How Can We Address Secularism and Other Destructive Trends in the World?

"Teach the people how to pray."
— POPE BENEDICT XVI TO U.S. BISHOPS IN APRIL 2008

One of the problems of secularism is the loss of important traditions — a tradition being the handing down of beliefs and customs from one generation to the next. At the heart of the life of the Church is the ability of the younger generations to receive these traditions from older and previous generations.

In a May 2004 Vatican meeting with American bishops visiting from the ecclesiastical provinces of San Antonio and Oklahoma City, Pope John Paul II recommended U.S. Catholics recover "devotions of popular piety" as a means of personal and communal sanctification. "For centuries the Holy Rosary, Stations of the Cross, prayer before and after meals, and other devotional practices have helped to form a school of prayer in families and parishes, acting as rich and beautiful supplements to the sacramental life of Catholics," he said.

"A renewal of these devotions will not only help the faithful in your country grow in personal holiness," he continued, "but will also act as a source of strength and sanctification for the Catholic Church in the United States."

It is up to us to pass on and to keep alive in our families the devotions, customs, and practices of our Catholic faith. The Church has always taught that parents are the primary educators of their children, and it is in the family that the faith is first transmitted and lived. We must make these spiritual investments for all future generations to ensure peace and truth for our own descendants.

To form kind and merciful hearts in their children, parents need to plant the seed of God and prayer in those young hearts. Plant the seed of reverence for the dead and in due time this will manifest itself and will assure you of their aid. Without those examples, children depart into godlessness.

Teach children about the meaning of All Souls Day. Teach them to go without what they enjoy (video games, for example), offer up what hurts (such as a skinned knee), and to accept what can be difficult for them (homework!). Teach them about the power of prayer and sacrifice. By praying for the souls of their deceased family, they make friends forever!

What's in It for Me?

What no eye has seen, nor ear heard, nor the heart of man conceived, what God has prepared for those who love him.
— 1 Corinthians 2:9

It is impossible to describe the gratitude the holy souls feel for those who help them. Filled with immense desire to repay the favors done them, they pray for you with a fervor so great, so intense, so constant, that God refuses them nothing. The souls become your powerful intercessors while you are on earth and pray for you when the time comes that your soul is in purgatory.

In addition, once they are released from purgatory, they prostrate themselves before the Throne of God — there are no ungrateful souls in heaven — and pray unceasingly for those who, through their prayers, helped release them from purgatory. By their prayers, they shield their friends from dangers and protect them from the evils that threaten them. They become our dearest, sincerest, and best friends forever.

On that glorious morning when Judgment Day dawns, a chorus of voices will rise in our behalf as those liberated souls cry out, "This priest, these sisters, this child, this man, this woman, freed us. We were in purgatory, and they descended among us to extinguish the purifying flames. They comforted us, and their suffrages opened our way to heaven. Grant them what they ask for, Lord. They have done great things for us."

Then Jesus will say to you, "Yes, I know what you have done, and I will remember it for all eternity. The Holy Spirit which I gave you did not return to me. The seed that was planted has borne fruit. You showed mercy, and mercy shall be yours. Blessed are the merciful for they shall receive mercy. 'Come, O blessed of my Father, inherit the kingdom prepared for you from the foundation of the world' "(Mt 25:34).

PART II
What Do the Saints Reveal About Purgatory?

"I felt great desires that the saints might pray for us, they who have so much power in their state of glory, and that the souls in purgatory might offer prayers for us amidst those remorseful lamentations of theirs.... These souls can do much for us (more than we can tell)."

— BLESSED PETER FAVRE

Throughout the centuries, the great saints of God have well understood the importance of praying for the souls in purgatory. It seems the Lord impressed on each of them his ardent desire that every possible spiritual help be given to these souls. No wonder the Church sees great merit in the saints' personal journeys which so often included coming to a better understanding of purgatory and, in some cases, having firsthand experiences of it. No wonder it encourages us to carefully study the lives of the saints to discover what purgatory meant for these holy ones and for their own faith.

The suffering souls are loved by the saints in heaven just as they were loved by them during their earthly pilgrimage, and even more so because in heaven the saints know better the souls' present misery and the indescribable glory for which they are destined. That is why the saints so strongly desire to see them released as soon as possible. This love and desire impelled the saints to pray tirelessly for their eternal rest. Many of them have made this devotion one of the strong characteristics of their own sanctity. We are being recruited to do the same.

In particular, these "holy patrons of the suffering souls" are solicitous for them, and pray to God to move charitable hearts on earth to bring these souls relief and release from the keen sufferings of purgatory. They encourage — and help us — to do that with the prayers, devotions, and practices they left for us so that we can lay up spiritual treasures for the suffering souls … and for ourselves.

God offers us the grace to avoid purgatory. He *wants* us to avoid it. That is his plan for us, which we can choose or reject. While on earth, one of the many ways we prepare ourselves for immediate entry into heaven is to pray for the souls now in purgatory. If we imitate the saints' devotion for these souls, then we, too, will merit receiving the aid of the saints' powerful intercession. And we will gain the intercession of those souls whom we helped free from purgatory and who are now members of the Church Triumphant in heaven.

The saints invite you now to descend in spirit into the silent and forgotten world of these suffering friends to learn wisdom from them. Visit them with your prayers and sacrifices. Appeal to them in the hour of trial and temptation; ask their intercession when facing difficult problems, and bring them the help they so desperately desire. Make *their* desire *your* desire: to see the face of God.

In this section, we will examine the role that purgatory and the suffering souls played in the lives of a select number of saints and how their experiences and forms of devotion can help us both become more aware of the souls in purgatory and release them from it.

Gregorian Masses and St. Gregory the Great: Champion of the Holy Souls

"We must live in such a way that we may deserve to take part in the everlasting Pasch."

— St. Gregory the Great

Gregorian Masses date back to the end of the sixth century when they were instituted by Pope St. Gregory the Great (d. 604), who had a keen interest in the afterlife, including recording accounts of near-death experiences. The Masses bear the name of this doctor of the Church because he established the practice while abbot of St. Andrew's Benedictine Abbey of Monte Coeli in Rome.

In one of his most notable works, called *Dialogues,* Pope Gregory wrote about the death of a monk named Justus. "See to it," he said, "that for thirty days the Holy Sacrifice of the Mass be offered for him and that not one day be missed in which the Holy Victim be immolated for his intention."

As abbot, Gregory loved his fellow community members but, at the same time, made sure each strictly followed the Rule of St. Benedict which governed the lives of the Benedictine monks.

That was why Abbot Gregory had Justus' body tossed on a garbage hill after three gold coins were found in the dead monk's cell: an article of the Rule prohibited *all* individual property. The money was thrown on the corpse in the presence of all the community members who, one by one, repeated the words of the apostle Peter to Simon the Magician found in Acts 8:20: "[Let your] silver perish with you."

Once this act was completed, mercy won over the heart of Abbot Gregory: He had the Holy Mass celebrated daily for thirty consecutive days for Justus' soul. (There is an inscription in the Church of SS. Andrew and Gregory — on the site of the sixth-century monastery — that notes those thirty Masses were offered there.) On the thirtieth day, the saint experienced a revelation telling him Justus was now in heaven and that thirty consecutive liturgies — which, all told, comprise the "Gregorian Masses" — were an effective way to free a soul from purgatory.

Pious tradition also says that when that thirtieth Mass concluded, Justus appeared to a fellow monk and told him, "Bless God, my dear brother, today I am delivered and admitted into the society of the saints."

Inflamed with an ardent charity for the purgatorial souls, Pope Gregory lamented that after his own death, he would not be able to do anything else for them. Tradition holds that Our Lord, aware of Gregory's concern, spoke to him and said, "My friend, I want to grant in your favor a privilege that will be unique. All souls in purgatory, for whom thirty Masses are offered in your honor and without interruption, will immediately be saved however great may be their debt toward me." This hallowed tradition of more than 1,300 years has been declared a "pious and reasonable belief of the faithful" on the authority of the Roman Curia.

Whom do you miss the most? For whom do you wish you could have done more? Who hurt you or others? Who had destructive patterns which have influenced you (e.g., perfectionism, fears, quick temper, etc.)? Who died without a feeling of being loved? Who has helped you develop your gifts in life? Who has helped you appreciate your family heritage? Have a Mass, or Gregorian Masses, offered for them! Put specific instructions in your will that Gregorian Masses be offered on your behalf.

(Another traditional practice — that has been traced back to apostolic times — is to offer Masses for your departed loved one on the third, seventh, and thirtieth days after death, and on the anniversary of his or her death. The Mass on the third day represents the Resurrection of Our Lord; the seventh day represents Sunday, the Sabbath, the day of rest; and the thirtieth day represents the numbers of days the Israelites mourned for Moses.)

Does offering thirty Gregorian Masses *always* rescue a soul from purgatory? Although the practice is approved by the Church, there is no official guarantee. Still, it is a custom that both underscores the power of the Holy Mass and reminds us that there are souls in purgatory who need our prayers.

Masses for the Living, Too

"Masses, Masses, these are what I need."
— BLESSED HENRY SUSO

Is a Mass offered for one who is still living more powerful than a Mass celebrated for that person after he or she has died? I often wondered about that, so I wrote to Father Edward McNamara, a noted Professor of Liturgy, at the Regina Apostolorum University in Rome. This is how he responded to my inquiry: *How can we say that one way of offering a Mass is "more powerful" than another?*

First of all, it is necessary to clarify that in itself the Mass has the same value of Christ's paschal mystery of which it is the ritual re-presentation. Therefore, its value is infinite, and one Mass is not more powerful than another. Thus, any difference in value must be sought in the effect on the person for whom the Sacrifice is being offered.

In the case of the deceased in purgatory any benefit is received passively, since the soul is no longer capable of performing new meritorious acts. While such a soul is already saved, it cannot increase in sanctity but only purify those imperfections which impede its definitive entrance into glory.

A living person, however, is still capable of growing in sanctifying grace. And so a Mass offered for a person already in God's grace has the effect of offering a gift of increased grace which the person may willingly receive in order to become more Christ-like.

As an intercessory prayer, a Mass offered for a person in a state of actual mortal sin may yet supply the grace necessary for repentance even though conversion is always a free acceptance of the grace that is offered.

While the Mass may be offered for other intentions as well (for instance, for those who are ill), I believe that the discourse regarding whether the Mass for the living is more powerful than for the dead lies principally in the above regarding the possible increase in sanctity. The offering of the Mass may also assist in this increase of sanctity by helping people face their sufferings and trials more deeply united to Christ.

Only the living can become holier, even to the point of directly entering heaven after death. Some might be perplexed by the idea that there can be differences in sanctity in heaven. The saints sometimes used a useful image to describe this possibility.

During life, by freely corresponding with grace, each person prepares his or her own capacity of being filled with God. In heaven, some will be like liqueur glasses; others, beer tankards; others, barrels; and a few oil tankers. The important thing is that all will be filled to the brim, and no one will feel the lack of anything necessary for happiness.

Of course, the Church recommends praying and having Masses offered for both the living and the dead, for none should be excluded from our charity.

— FATHER EDWARD MCNAMARA,
LETTER OF JUNE 5, 2007

While we often hear of Masses being said for the dead, it is time to realize that a Mass offered for the intention of the living can have extraordinary effects while they are still on earth.

In the early twentieth century, Pope Benedict XV (d. 1922) wrote: "Why do not the faithful, who wish to secure a rich and holy death, have Holy Mass celebrated for that intention? Applied to the living, the fruits of the Holy Sacrifice are much more copious than when applied to the dead. Their application to the former — their intention and their dispositions to be as they ought — is more direct, more certain and more abundant than their disposition to the latter."

The simple lesson is: *Pray for the living now.* Pray for their eternity. You will help them — and yourselves.

As we face life's struggles here on earth, there are special graces, and many can come from a Mass for the living. When we have Masses said regularly for ourselves, loved ones, and friends during life, this translates into the source of actual graces that can help:

- Urge a soul to repentance.
- Lead an individual to a more fervent prayer life.
- Enable a person to persevere against the Evil One and the dangers of our world.
- Grow in the ability to believe in love of God and of neighbor. (Asking for this "choice" grace is a particularly potent prayer.)

The way is open for us to make progress in virtue, to acquire merit, and to augment our degree of glory in heaven — all by having Masses offered while we are still alive. We have in the Holy Sacrifice of the Mass, then, a real means of assuring for ourselves a good and holy death *if we place no voluntary obstacle in the way!*

You may have arranged for having Masses said for you after you have died, but do not wait till then for the graces that are available for you. Divine Justice is less exacting before death than after. Have a Mass offered from time to time for the special intention of your sanctification and perseverance in grace. And tend to loved ones! That simple, thoughtful act is a means of surrounding ourselves in eternity with many grateful friends.

The old maxim "charity begins at home" is a wise and commendable one when it comes to the hereafter, and if we act on it, we ensure ourselves, and our loved ones, a more prompt release from purgatory.

So when a birthday, anniversary, holy day, or holiday comes along, ask for a Holy Mass or Mass Enrollment to be offered for you and do the same for others. It may be done now, in the dark of this earth, but it will follow you into the light to heaven!

Come, Let Us Worship the Lord

"Christ is the victim, which gives solace to the dead."
— St. John Chrysostom

St. John Chrysostom (d. 407) often wrote about the relationship between the Mass and the souls in purgatory and said it was not in vain that the apostles enjoined the dead in the Eucharistic Prayer. They knew the great benefit the souls would derive from this.

Tracing liturgical prayer for the dead back to the apostles, this Church Father pointed out: "The apostles knew full well that it works much good for the departed: for whenever all the people stand with hands raised in prayer, together with the whole assembly of the priests, and the tremendous Victim lies on the altar, should we not by our petitions in their behalf move the heart of God?"

He also encouraged those who were weeping over the deaths of their loved ones to turn to the Holy Eucharist and offer prayers, alms, and sacrifices for them instead of tears alone.

Another Church Father, St. Augustine, wrote: "There is no doubt that the dead received help through prayers of the Church and through the Holy Sacrifice of the Mass."

In our own time, daily and hourly, Jesus renews the offering of himself on our altars, that we may live to eternity and that the holy souls may be liberated. Let us frequently receive Holy Communion and assist at Holy Mass for the benefit of those pining in purgatory. How anxiously they must watch as Mass is offered, seeking the assurance of the prayers for the dead which will contribute to the end of their sufferings.

How often do we forget our holy dead once they are buried? (Purgatory is like a lost continent: "out of sight, out of mind.") So preoccupied with our own problems and needs, how often do we make almost mindless prayers, which if applied to the suffering souls, would bring an ocean of soothing relief to their pains? (Communion received without any special intention, for example, which — if offered for them— may be the final support needed to complete their term of banishment!)

St. Jane de Chantal (d. 1641) thought she could pray with more recollection in the quiet of her own room rather than in the church. Her spiritual director, St. Francis de Sales (d. 1622), explained that assistance at Holy Mass and prayers before the Blessed Sacrament in the tabernacle were of far greater profit than private devotions. In the same way, joining in the prayers of the Mass, spending time before the Blessed Sacrament, and saying the Rosary publicly on behalf of the purgatorial souls is preferred to practicing private acts of piety for the souls' sake.

Let us ask the holy angels to help us in our love of the Blessed Sacrament! Let us remember the holy souls whenever we are worshiping before Our Lord in the Eucharist! We will contribute to the glory of God by playing a role in helping the souls come into his presence in the heavenly court. And our own fervor and devotion — fortified by the gratitude of the holy souls — will increase.

"O Sacrament most Holy! O Sacrament divine! All praise and all thanksgiving be every moment Thine!"

Why Souls Are Called Both "Poor" and "Holy"

"Have pity on me, have pity on me, O you my friends.
— Job 19:21

In this "valley of tears" (and sighs), our sufferings can be particularly meritorious, especially if offered to God in atonement for sin. It is much better to cancel our debt now, since we can do it at far less a cost to ourselves and at the same time increase our eternal reward.

(If our sins are forgiven at confession what debt do we still owe? Although our offenses are forgiven, we must make "satisfaction" for them. This is why the priest gives us a penance to perform. It can consist of prayer, an offering, voluntary self-denial, sacrifices, patient acceptance of the cross we must bear, or one of the works of mercy. For more on the works of mercy, see CCC 2447.)

One thing that the holy souls look forward to is the Beatific Vision: seeing the One they desire. Their greatest consolation is the absolute certainty of salvation. Their greatest source of joy — through the pains of purgatory — is submission to God. They know their sins must be atoned for (which they are unable to do for themselves in purgatory), but theirs is an agreeable conformity to God's will.

However... their suffering continues without any alleviation or interruption.

We call these souls "poor" because they are expiating. They are being purged. They are "making recompense." How painful that can be! They realize as they never did on earth the blessedness of possessing God, of loving him totally, of always seeking him, which causes them to endure the bitterness of "hope deferred [that] makes the heart sick" (Prov 13:12). They are "poor" because they are in the most dreadful state of poverty: the loss of the sight of God.

For that reason it would be well for us if we learn to love God *now*. Love will teach us to do penance for our faults against him, and then we will not have to lament: "Woe is me, that my sojourning is prolonged" (Ps 119:5, Douay-Rheims). The late Mother St. Austin, from the Order of the Helpers of the Holy Souls, captures it: "Happy are those who do not wait for purgatory to repay the immense riches of God with the only riches in their power — the love of their whole heart, mind, soul and strength."

The souls are called "holy" at the same time as they are called "poor" because they can no longer sin. They are unspeakably holy. *They are confirmed in grace.* What a joy it must be amid their sufferings to know they can never again turn away from God! They are free from all sinful affection and everything that leads to it. Sin is now one thing they abhor. Its cruel consequences still are a source of intense loathing and anguish. The "holy" ones love God with great intensity and are inexpressibly dear to him.

It's said that the sister of St. Malachy (d. 1148) was so worldly minded that her brother did not see her for as long as she lived. However, after her death a voice told him his sister was at the door, complaining that she had had nothing to eat for thirty days. The saint understood what "food" she was seeking because it had been exactly thirty days since he had offered the sacrifice of the Living Bread — the Eucharist — for her. He again offered Mass for her benefit and soon saw her in a lighter garment and then, once more, clad entirely in white and surrounded by the saints. (It was St. Bernard who commented, "See what the continued prayer of the just can do!")

True Christians mourn their friends not in a vain hope but with a prayerful appeal at Mass to the Throne of Mercy. The Holy Sacrifice of the Mass has infinite value that we will never be able to comprehend until we are on the other side with the perspective of the angels!

Ways We Can Avoid Purgatory

"Divine Providence always provides in every life the purification that is needed to allow us to go straight to heaven."
— St. John of the Cross

Purgatory is an emergency entrance to heaven for those who have wasted grace on earth. What God considered the exception became the rule, and the rule — to go straight to heaven — has become the exception.

To avoid purgatory is to honor, to magnify, the redemption of Christ. As St. Paul teaches, "Where sin increased, grace abounded all the more" (Rom 5:20). Let us show God our gratitude and take advantage of the great opportunities of paying our debt in this life.

How can we avoid purgatory?

- First and foremost, do the will of God in all things. True love consists in carrying out God's holy will.
- Avoid sin at all cost, especially mortal sins and deliberate venial sins. (A little girl was asked about sin. She said, "Mortal sin makes God angry, venial sin makes him nervous!")
- Break off all poor habits.
- Go to monthly confession. Go to daily Mass. Pray the Rosary daily. Pray more and chatter less! *Pray. Pray. Pray.* (We must return to the Upper Room and rediscover the

power of prayer.) Be alone with God and speak to him from your heart. We are all invited to say "Yes, thy will be done."

- Remember, too, that we all have our own "purgatory" while we are here on earth. The difference is how we choose to embrace it. Offer up everyday crosses. When we suffer, we have a great chance to show God that we love him.

- Make sacrifices and acts of self-denial.

- Go to Eucharistic Adoration. Love and adore our precious Jesus who is waiting for you to give you many special graces. His heart breaks from the sins of our poor world. Go and comfort, adore, and kneel before the Lord, our God, in reparation for the sins of the world and for the dying and the souls in purgatory.

- Read Scripture, the living Word of God. It is our foundation. Christ lives in the Scriptures. Take a passage each day and remember that passage throughout the day to guide you. (Pope Benedict XVI recommends the ancient practice of *Lectio divina:* "The diligent reading of Sacred Scripture accompanied by prayer brings about that intimate dialogue in which the person reading hears God who is speaking, and in praying, responds with trusting openness of heart (cf. *Dei Verbum,* n. 25)." The pontiff is convinced this practice will bring to the Church a spiritual springtime!)

Follow the advice of St. Thérèse of Lisieux (d. 1897): "Do many little things." Perform acts of kindness. Even the smallest things out of love please God.

- Accept trials, pain, and death. Endure like the holy souls.

- Avoid judging others. Be patient. Do not overreact.

- Forgive. Forgive. Forgive. Only forgiving souls make it to purgatory.
- Value the Church's gift of indulgences.

A message that God asks of us is the heart of the message of Fátima: "Pray and offer sacrifices to the Most High." Sister Lucia, one of the three visionaries, elaborates:

> Endure uncomplainingly, whatever little annoyances we may encounter on our path. Sometimes it may be disagreeable, irritating or an unpleasant word. It may be a misunderstanding, a reproof, a rejection, or an act of ingratitude.
>
> It is necessary to know how to endure all things offering our sacrifice to God and letting things drop as if we were deaf, dumb, and blind. Repay those with a smile, a kind deed, a favor, forgiving and loving, with our eyes fixed on God. *The fruit of our sacrifices is so that we may see better, speak with greater certainty and hear the voice of God.*

What a grace! This denial, Sister Lucia adds, "is often the most difficult for our human nature, but it is also the one most pleasing to God and meritorious for ourselves."

Listen!

"Let us ask three graces of Jesus. To avoid Purgatory. To learn from Purgatory. To empty Purgatory."
— Blessed James Alberione

One of the surest means of avoiding purgatory is to aid the suffering souls in whatever way we can. We can better do that if we *listen* with our hearts because:

- Among the voices crying out may be that of your own earthly father. "My child," he asks, "have you forgotten me? When I laid my hand in blessing on your head for the last time, you promised me never to forget me and to pray for me. For a long time your faithful prayers descended upon me like refreshing dew. You gave me a share in many holy Masses. Why are your prayers becoming so rare?"

- You may "hear" your own mother. "Have mercy on me, for I am lonely and poor!" she says. "So long, oh, so long, have I waited for you, my child, but you never come. How many tears you shed for me at my death. Surely your heart has not turned from me now?" How is it that you seldom bring me a greeting, a consolation, a gift of love? Oh, my child, whom I bore beneath my heart, for whom I sighed even in death, I think of you unceasingly even in my suffering. Do not abandon me now. Outstretch your hand to help me out of these torments. Lead me to God and into eternal rest and peace!"

- There are others begging for your help: "Have mercy on us for we are lonely and poor!" Whose voices are these? Your brother is among them. Your sister, your husband, your wife, your pastor, your bishop, those who have helped you in life. They lament, and they plead: "Forget us not. To be forgotten is so hard. Remember us, but not with empty reminiscences. Become our deliverers, and we will become your powerful intercessors forever."

If we must burn, let it be with the fire of love now, not with the purifying flames in the hereafter.

The Motto of Blessed Mary of Providence: "Prayer, Suffering, Work"

"Oh! If all of us but knew how great is the power of the good souls in purgatory with the heart of God, and if we knew all the graces we can obtain through their intercession, they would not be so much forgotten! We must pray much for them, so that they may pray much for us."

— St. John Vianney

"Prayer, Suffering, Work, for the Holy Souls in Purgatory" was the motto of Blessed Mary of Providence (d. 1871), foundress of the Society of Helpers of the Holy Souls.

Charity for the souls in purgatory is one of the most touching characteristics of our Catholic faith. From the earliest ages of Christianity, prayers and good works have been offered for the dead, bonding the Church Militant on earth with the Church Suffering in purgatory.

However, it was not until the mid-nineteenth century that a special religious community was created for the relief and deliverance of the faithful departed through spiritual and temporal works of mercy.

Founded with the special purpose of assisting the holy souls in purgatory by the various means which God has revealed, this religious institute of women rose during a providential epoch. In a century very much like our own — where material interests and indifference alternated with unbelief — the ancient practices of prayers and Masses for the dead had, for the most part, been sadly forgotten.

As one priest noted: "When God intends to manifest that he is, so to speak, the original Author of any special work, often he writes his cipher on some lowly heart which the world ignores; he comes suddenly and foreshadows to it some indication of his will, the full meaning of which will not be clearly unfolded, until the divinely chosen hour shall have arrived for its executions."

So it was with the origin of the Helpers of the Holy Souls, a group that existed only as a pious idea in the heart of a young girl destined to be its foundress: Eugénie-Marie-Joseph Smet (Blessed Mary of Providence), who as a little girl had puzzled playmates with remarks like: *"The souls are in prison, a fire, but the Good God asks us only for a prayer to let them out and we don't say it."*

As a young woman, Eugénie once commented to an archbishop, "Day and night I am pursued by the same thought: One does not pray enough for the dead. Hundreds of thousands of people die every day. *Where is there a community devoted exclusively to the relief and deliverance of these dear souls?"*

She set out to change that, and St. John Vianney, the Curé d'Ars, encouraged her, telling Sister Mary that doing what she planned was the will of God and "a realization of the love of the Sacred Heart of Jesus."

Those words were lodged within her like a burning brand, and with five companions she pronounced her vows and launched her special apostolate in Paris on December 27, 1856. She offered herself as victim of expiation for these souls. All her prayers, all her mortifications, all her heroic acts were offered for them. As she said: "I would like to empty purgatory with one hand, and with the other to fill it with souls snatched from the brink of hell."

Blessed Mary of Providence had wonderful nuggets of great wisdom and insight, including:

- "Let us make no other projects than to do God's will. If the souls in purgatory could exchange places with us, how gladly they would suffer, and how slight our sufferings seem to them! Those who cannot suffer cannot love."
- "Before we can follow the martyrs to distant lands, however, we must vigorously accept daily martyrdom of minute sacrifices. If we only knew what benefit it procured for the souls in purgatory."
- "The souls in purgatory suffer without a moment's interruption. Their helpers must never cease a moment to assist them. How could we think of rest on earth?"
- "Fear nothing except not to do the perfect Will of God. The good Lord will contrive to weave a crown for you out of all the nothings you have offered up for His love."
- "The heart of a helper, so close to purgatory, must always be on fire."

Let us pray that we may never be grouped with those whom St. Bernard describes as producing "much weeping but no fruit, and who are more to be pitied themselves than the dead whose loss they mourn!"

Be Greedy and Grab the Grace of Indulgences

"Indulgences are of such value that I find myself unable to appreciate them according to their true worth or to speak of them highly enough. Thus I exhort you to hold them in the highest possible esteem."

— St. Ignatius of Loyola

St. Joseph Cafasso (d. 1860) was called a "glutton for indulgences" as a means for both avoiding purgatory himself and for helping the souls in purgatory speedily attain heaven. We, too, must be greedy for grace for the holy souls. We must pray to live and die in the state of grace. We must pray to avoid purgatory. We must become a "glutton" for spiritual sacrifices.

Exactly what is an indulgence? The word itself comes from the Latin *indulgentia* which means to be kind or tender. Quoting Pope Paul VI's apostolic constitution *Indulgentiarum Doctrina* and the Code of Canon Law, the *Catechism of the Catholic Church* (1471) defines it this way:

"An indulgence is a remission before God of the temporal punishment due to sins whose guilt has already been forgiven, which the faithful Christian who is duly disposed gains under certain prescribed conditions through the action of the Church which, as the minister of redemption, dispenses and applies with authority the treasury of the satisfactions of Christ and the saints."

"An indulgence is partial or plenary according as it removes either part or all of the temporal punishment due to sin." The faithful can gain indulgences for themselves or apply them to the dead.

Because God lavishes his mercy on us, we have a treasure house of indulgences to be gained for our souls and the souls of our beloved dead including pious invocations, individual short and long prayers, litanies, the Rosary, and the use of objects of devotion in prayer. We also have specific actions or activities, such as saying the Stations of the Cross, renewing our baptismal vows at Easter, singing special hymns, visiting cemeteries, and teaching Christian doctrine. In addition, there are special occasions or events for the faithful, including papal blessings, Eucharistic processions, public novenas, and pilgrimages. The list goes on and on.

Why do we have indulgences? Their purpose is to make up for penances omitted, poorly done, or too light in comparison with the enormity of the sins. Archbishop Fulton Sheen explained: "It is like a nail in a board. Once you remove the nail — the sin — with confession, the hole which is the punishment remains to be filled. How is that hole to be filled? By penance and reparation." Indulgences fill that hole on earth by fulfilling a person's need to atone for the harm they have caused to themselves and to others.

Indulgences arise from the mercy of Jesus; that is, with them we can satisfy our debts. They are an aid for growth toward spiritual perfection, inner change, or a deeper conversion of heart. They are not a discount for performing outward acts. The appropriate inner disposition is required to benefit from indulgences.

In the words of Venerable John Henry Newman (d. 1890): "The smallest venial sin rocks the foundations of the created world." That is, even our smallest sins can have a ripple effect that travels great distances and influences many lives. However, through God's grace, the holiness even of the lowliest saint far exceeds the harm even the greatest sinner can do. The graces won by Christ and the saints are an inexhaustible treasure that can be used to heal the wounds of the world. God desires us to use this spiritual treasury to move us closer to him in this life and to prepare our souls to be with him in the next.

In granting indulgences the Church does a holy and whole-some thing. It acts according to the merciful spirit of Jesus who was all compassion for poor sinners. It was Our Lord who gave us the first indulgence. On the cross he atoned for the sins of all mankind. The Church fulfills a command for reconciling man with God. It is a defined doctrine that the Church can grant indulgences. What a marvelous privilege we have in indulgences. They are a concrete sign of God's tender, loving mercy!

In fact, at the death of a pontiff the only office at the Vatican whose duties do not cease is that of the Apostolic Penitentiary. It is a tribunal of mercy responsible for issues relating to the forgive-ness of sins in the Church. That branch of the Holy See is respon-sible for assuring God's people of mercy. God's mercy endures forever! His mercy is available to us at all times in all circum-stances. It never ceases. We only have to avail ourselves of it.

We can do this "repair work" here on earth or in purgatory. By going to confession regularly, one can gain many plenary indulgences, thereby healing all the effects of one's sins. So solici-tous was St. Alphonsus Liguori (d. 1787) about gaining indul-gences that, after his death, several "indulgenced" articles were found on him. The saint had always carried such sacramentals and prayers wherever he went in order to gain as many indul-gences as possible. We ourselves have many debts with God, and many souls await our charity. What more do we need to motivate us? Our ability to gain indulgences so readily ought to make us eager, busy bees.

Another wonderful example is St. Mary Magdalene de Pazzi (d. 1607). After a member of her religious congregation passed away, St. Mary was not content that only the usual prayers for the dead be said for her. Instead, the community also applied to the departed soul the holy indulgences they had gained that day. In a vision, the saint saw the sister's soul ascending toward heaven to receive the crown of glory.

"Farewell, Sister!" St. Mary exclaimed. While she was speaking, Jesus appeared to console her, declaring it was because of the indulgences that this soul had been so swiftly released from purgatory and admitted into paradise. As a result, a fervor for gaining indulgences was enkindled within that particular convent.

May a spark of that same holy fervor be lit in our own hearts and fanned into a bright flame!

The Great Pardon: The Portiuncula Indulgence

"O my Brothers and Sisters, I want you all to go to heaven!"
— St. Francis of Assisi

The Portiuncula (a word that means "small portion") refers to the land in Assisi in the time of St. Francis of Assisi (d. 1226). The property belonged to the Benedictines and included a dilapidated church dedicated to the Blessed Virgin Mary. Francis, who had great devotion to the Queen of the World, saw the church was deserted and in desperate need of repair. He went to work begging in the streets and crying out: "He who gives me a stone shall have one blessing; he who gives me two stones shall have two." He heard that the chapel was called Our Lady of the Angels because angels frequently appeared there.

The Benedictines wanted to give Francis the property, but in order for him to remain faithful to Lady Poverty, he rented it from them with the annual compensation of a basket of fish from the Tescio River. The church and land became the cradle of the three orders he founded, was where he received St. Clare as his spiritual daughter, and was where he died, commending this spot above all others to the friars as a place most dear to the Blessed Virgin.

The saint had a most tender compassion for all men and a wonderful love for poverty. He prayed most especially, with tears and groans, for the conversion of sinners.

On a night in July 1216, Francis was at prayer in the little church of the Portiuncula, devoured by love for God and a thirst to save souls. He prayed for the forgiveness of sins of mankind.

Suddenly a brilliant light shone all around. In great splendor Jesus and Mary appeared in the midst of a dazzling cloud surrounded by a multitude of radiant angels. Out of fear and reverence, Francis adored Our Lord, prostrating himself on the ground. Then Jesus said to him: *"Francis you are very zealous for the good souls. Ask me what you want for their salvation."* St. Francis was rapt in ecstasy before Our Lord. When he regained his courage, he said: "Lord, I, a miserable sinner, beg you to concede an indulgence to all those who enter this church, who are truly contrite and have confessed their sins. And I beg Blessed Mary, your mother, intercessor of man, that she intercede on behalf of this grace."

The Merciful Virgin at once began to beseech her Son on behalf of Francis. Jesus answered: "It is a very great thing you ask me; but you are worthy of even greater things, Friar Francis, and greater things you will have. So I accept your request, but I want you to go to my vicar, to whom I have given the power to bind and loose in heaven and on earth, to ask him on my behalf for this indulgence."

With one of his companions Francis hastened to Pope Honorius III, fell prostrate before him, and implored the pontiff to proclaim that everyone visiting the church and confessing their sins with a contrite heart would be as pure from all sin and punishments as he was immediately after baptism. The pope granted this petition, and this indulgence has been extended to all parish churches throughout the world for one day each year.

The date has been set from noon on August 1 until midnight on August 2, the feast of Our Lady of the Angels. It is said that Francis was given this day by Our Lord because of the feast of the Chains of St. Peter, celebrated on August 1, commemorating Peter's being released from prison and his chains removed. This is an extraordinary demonstration of God's mercy in removing the chains of sin from those who devoutly and faithfully seek to gain the indulgence by completing its requirements.

The conditions to obtain the Plenary Indulgence of the Forgiveness of Assisi (for oneself or for a departed soul) are as follows:

- Sacramental confession (during eight days before or after).
- Participation in the Mass and Eucharist.
- Recitation of the Apostles' Creed, Our Father, and a prayer for the pope's intention.

In the thirteenth century, it was revealed to St. Margaret of Cortona that the souls in purgatory eagerly look forward every year to the feast of Our Lady of the Angels because it is a day of deliverance for a great number of them.

The Portiuncula Indulgence is a grace not to be missed, not only for yourself but for the many souls suffering in purgatory. Circle your calendar for the feast of Our Lady of the Angels beginning at noon on August 1. Tell everyone of the magnitude of this grace. Once again, we see the unfathomable Divine Mercy of God.

Giving Alms and the Release of Souls

Water extinguishes a blazing fire: so almsgiving atones for sin.

— SIRACH 3:30

God calls us to give. Such offerings help us to grow in love for him and our neighbor. The giving of alms has been considered a most satisfactory work of penance for the holy souls. "For almsgiving delivers from death, and it will purge away every sin," said the angel to Tobit (Tb 12:9). Offered for the dead, giving alms possesses a triple effect. It enriches the giver with merit, aids the poor, and mitigates or even delivers the soul from purgatory. God the Father faithfully recompenses generosity toward those who are in need with a blessing of peace, inner satisfaction, and joy.

Almsgiving is one of the surest means of anticipating our own purgatorial debt, thus assuring speedy entrance into heaven. Like any act of charity, however, our almsgiving must be done with purity of intention in a spirit of charity. God does not so much regard the amount of alms given as he does the heart of the one who gives it. Our charity must be commensurate with our means.

Spiritual alms are at the disposal of all. At the forefront are voluntary penances great and small: fasting, occasional self-denial of the smallest luxuries of life, physical sufferings, disappointments, bereavement, poverty, and so forth. Everyone has something to give to our suffering friends.

We gain grateful friendship of those whom we have relieved in their suffering. They will aid us in working out our own salvation. When we pay their debts and deliver them from the detention of purgatory, we give them the object of their desire: to enjoy the everlasting presence of God. That's heaven!

St. Gregory Nazianzen said, "Nothing can win the love of God like alms, because goodness and compassion are the most distinctive characteristics of the Divinity." Whoever aids God is assured of paradise.

We should not be afraid of exercising charity toward the suffering souls. St. Ambrose said, "Whatever we offer in charity for the dead is changed into merit for ourselves, and we shall receive a hundredfold after death." When St. John of God collected alms for the hospital in the streets of Granada, he called out: "Give alms, my brothers and sisters, for the love and mercy of yourselves." He did not say: "Pity the poor sick!" He said: "Be merciful to yourselves!" (I call out to you: Be good to the holy souls, out of mercy towards them, and out of mercy towards yourselves.)

St. John Chrysostom beautifully adds:

> Alms is a heavenly work, and most many-sided of all good works. It protects those who practice it. It is the friend of God, and powerful in obtaining grace for those whom

it loves. It breaks the chains, dispels the darkness, extinguishes the fire. It approaches, and the gates of the Kingdom open fully to it. When a Queen comes, no guard dare to question her right to enter, but all would hasten to open wide the gates. So it is with alms for she is a Queen and she knows how to make men like unto God.

She has wings and she flies easily; golden wings that glance in the light of heaven, rejoicing the angels. She is always near to the Throne of God, and when we appear before the tribunal of the sovereign Judge, she flies to meet us, and covers us with the protection of her wings.

The words of Malachi where God tells us to "put me to the test" (Mal 3:10) encourage us to give alms as a part of our spiritual and financial life. The blessings the Lord has in store for us on behalf of the holy souls are endless.

During the Month of Souls, Recall Gertrude the Great

"The number is proportionate to the zeal and fervor of those who pray for them!"

— JESUS' ANSWER TO ST. GERTRUDE WHEN
SHE ASKED HOW MANY SOULS WERE RELEASED
FROM PURGATORY BY HER SISTERS' PRAYERS

When it comes to rescuing souls in purgatory, one has to mention the great St. Gertrude.

St. Gertrude was born in Eisleben, Thuringia, Germany, in 1256. As a young girl she was placed in the care of the Benedictine nuns at Rodalsdorf, where she became a nun in the same monastery and was elected abbess in 1251.

St. Gertrude dedicated herself to the pursuit of perfection and gave herself over to prayer and contemplation. She was gifted with high intellectual capabilities along with being able to read and converse in Latin. Her devotion to her literary pursuits were the best and purest kind: Scripture, the Church Fathers, and other theological works.

St. Gertrude began to have supernatural visions and mystical experiences at the age of twenty-six, and she received many powerful teachings. She wrote a series of prayers that became very popular and through her writings helped spread devotion to the Sacred Heart. She meditated on the Passion of Christ, which many times brought a flood of tears to her eyes. She had a tender love for Our Lady. Her life and revelations record many conversations with Our Lord where he reveals his great desire to grant mercy to souls to reward the least good act.

Gertrude's heart reached out to all. Her boundless charity embraced rich and poor, learned and simple. It was also manifested in her tenderness and sympathy toward the poor souls in purgatory.

With regard to suffering, Our Lord said to her: "When man, after applying the remedy for his suffering, patiently bears for love of me that which he is unable to cure, he gains a glorious prize."

Regarding frequent Communion, Jesus told Gertrude: "Those who have received me often on earth shall be more glorious in heaven. At each Communion, I increase, I multiply the riches which are to constitute the Christian's happiness in heaven!"

Other visions expressed Our Lord's wishes for people to pray for the souls in purgatory. He once showed Gertrude a table of gold, on which were many costly pearls. The pearls were prayers for the holy souls. At the same time, the saint had a vision of souls freed from suffering and ascending in the form of bright sparks in different shapes to heaven.

In another vision, Our Lord told St. Gertrude that he longs for someone to ask him to release souls from purgatory. Jesus said to St. Gertrude, "By the prayers of thy loving souls, I am induced to free a 'prisoner' from purgatory as often as you move your tongue to utter a word of prayer."

On another day, St. Gertrude asked Our Lord how many souls his mercy would release from purgatory, and he replied that his love desires to release *all* souls from purgatory. He encouraged her to pray with confident assurance and to ask more than she dare for their release. (In other words, Our Lord is telling us to pray with zeal and fervor, to ASK BIG, to BE BOLD.)

In another vision, St. Gertrude was given the following prayer which Our Lord told her would release 1,000 souls from purgatory every time it is said with love and devotion:

Eternal Father, I offer you the Most Precious Blood of Thy Divine Son, Jesus, in union with the Masses said throughout the world today, for all the Holy Souls in purgatory, for sinners everywhere, those in the Universal Church, in my home and in my own family. Amen.

Are 1,000 souls really released from purgatory?

Theologians tell us we may not be certain of the exact number. However, the number 1,000 is biblical and symbolic for infinite. We do know that Our Lord points to the efficacy of our prayers offered up for these suffering souls. A "thousand" souls released means more than we can count, more than we dare to ask.

St. Gertrude's feast day is November 16. She is called "Great" because of her love for the Sacred Heart and the beloved souls in purgatory.

Tradition tells us that the most souls are released on Christmas Day, not All Souls Day. In honor of St. Gertrude, we can ask Our Lord to *empty* purgatory not only on Christmas but every day. Let us ask more than we dare. Let us be BOLD in our asking. Let us give these saintly sufferers to Our Lord all year round.

What a glorious day in heaven it will be for everyone when purgatory is no more!

St. Nicholas and His Gift of Saving Souls

For those whom he foreknew he also predestined to be conformed to the image of his Son.

— Romans 8:29

It is a treasure of a story, connected right to the afterlife. It involves St. Nicholas of Tolentino. The story: St. Nicholas's parents Compagnone and Amata, who were neither from a noble family nor rich, wanted to have children but were unable to conceive.

In fervent prayer, they made this promise through the aid of another "Nicholas," St. Nicholas of Bari. "If God, through your intercession, would grant us a son, we would be very pleased if he would want to become a religious; if however, it would be a girl, may she become a cloistered nun."

Having made such a promise, the parents went on pilgrimage to Bari, south of Italy, and then returned to Castel Sant' Angelo, their native town. Nine months later a son they named Nicholas was born to them.

This was 1245. The couple was loved and respected by the people, and many predictions circulated about their new child, obviously a special one.

At an early age Nicholas was attracted by the preaching of an Augustinian friar, Father Reginaldo, prior of the monastery in Sant' Angelo. One day he heard him preaching this Gospel passage, "Love not the world, nor the things that are in the world.... The world is passing away."

Deeply moved, Nicholas asked to be admitted to the community, where he gave himself to prayer and works of penance with such intensity that it was at times necessary for his superiors to impose limitations on him.

Nicholas was ordained to the priesthood in 1271, served in various monasteries, and was esteemed by all. He spent the last thirty years of his life in Tolentino, dedicating his innocence to the altar with great devotion, sincerity, and humility. He was a joy to those who were sad, a consolation to the suffering, support for the poor, and a healing balm for prisoners, especially the imprisoned of purgatory.

People had a great confidence in Nicholas' prayers on behalf of the faithful departed. He prayed for the holy souls six to eight hours a night! It was before the Blessed Sacrament that St. Nicholas most loved to pray. There he spent long hours, chiefly petitioning relief for the souls of the faithful departed. One Saturday night, the soul of a deceased fellow Augustinian, Pellegrino of Osimo, appeared to Nicholas, begging him: "I am presently burning in these flames where our good God, accepting my repentance, is mercifully purifying me. I beg you to celebrate a Mass for the Dead, so that I may be freed from these sufferings." However, Nicholas was under obedience to offer the community Mass of the Order for the next week.

Brother Pellegrino's soul continued: "My Father, come with me and you will understand how urgent it is to satisfy the requests of the innumerable souls who sent me to you to beg to you."

And suddenly the valley of Pesaro appeared to Nicholas as if transformed into burning fire. Before him were souls of every age and condition. The holy priest wept. Brother Pellegrino implored, "Have mercy, Father Nicholas, on this wretched multitude of souls! If you will celebrate a Mass for their suffrage, most of them will be freed from these sufferings."

Early the next morning Father Nicholas shared his vision with the prior, and he, too, broke down into tears. The prior approved his request, and after Father Nicholas had offered Masses, said prayers, and done penance for a week, the soul of Brother Pellegrino appeared to him to thank him and assure him that his and the other souls were freed from purgatory. They called him their "liberator."

St. Nicholas died on September 10, 1305. His remains are preserved in the sanctuary that bears his name at Tolentino. His feast is observed on the day of his death. To this day, a daily Mass for the Dead is celebrated there for the souls in purgatory.

At the altar of the shrine is a painting depicting the saint celebrating Mass for the holy souls, along with his vision of souls being released from purgatory during Mass.

In 1884, Pope Leo XIII proclaimed St. Nicholas "Patron of the Souls in Purgatory," and dedicated the Basilica of St. Nicholas-Church of the Poor Souls in Purgatory.

St. Nicholas of Tolentino, pray for us!

St. John Macias' Powerful Aid

We must work... while it is day; night comes, when no one can work.

— JOHN 9:4

Thank God the bright light of day is still shining for us. There is still time when we can work, when nothing is done in vain and everything we do has merit!

Juan (John) Macias was born in southwestern Spain on March 2, 1585. His parents were of noble lineage but impoverished. They were blessed with two children, Juan and Ines. Orphaned at the age of four, the children were adopted by a kind uncle for whom John tended sheep. One day while he was watching the grazing flock, a heavenly youth appeared before him.

"I am John the Evangelist, and I come from heaven," said the apparition.

"Who is John the Evangelist?" inquired the startled youth.

"He is the beloved disciple of the Lord. I am here because God has chosen you for himself. I am to take you to distant lands. God sent me to be your companion."

The youth cried with joy: "God's will be done! I only want to do God's will!"

Leaving Spain, John Macias traveled throughout South America working at various jobs. He ultimately arrived in Lima, Peru, where he would remain the rest of his life.

Macias entered the Dominican monastery of La Magdalena, where he was professed as a lay brother. Like other great saints, he was assigned as porter. He lived a life of prayer and penance, served from two to six Masses daily, and spent his leisure time before the Blessed Sacrament.

Our Lady taught this holy doorkeeper the sublime mysteries of the Rosary. It was through the most powerful Marian prayer on earth, the Rosary, that he would release great numbers of souls in purgatory. And thus his biographers labeled Macias the "Helper of the Poor Souls."

Souls often appeared to St. John begging his powerful intercession. One night, as he was praying in the Rosary chapel, he heard the murmur of many confused and hoarse voices.

"Oh Servant of God, remember us! Do not forget us! Help us with your prayers so that we may leave this place of suffering," were some of the cries. "Who are you?" inquired John. "We are the souls in purgatory. Commend us to God! Commend us to God!" came a mournful chorus. John saw a number of shadowy figures advancing out of the darkness. They seemed to him like a hive of bees whose whispers and sighs were pleading for relief.

Eyes filled with tears and arms outstretched, they desperately pleaded, "Give us prayers! Oh, Brother John, you are the friend of the poor and sick! Be our friend, too! Help make us worthy to be with God and his blessed ones!"

The lay brother stared in awe. Hundreds of women and children were grouped about the main altar. And every face was marked with loneliness and pain, their greatest longing that of entering heaven without further delay.

His heart was moved with compassion. Brother John recited the Rosary with even greater devotion. Every night he offered three Rosaries for them, praying on his knees despite his fatigue. These three Rosaries were offered for all the souls in purgatory, the souls of deceased priests and religious, and for deceased relatives, friends, and benefactors. He also offered for all the suffering souls half of his Communions, all the indulgences he could gain, and the twenty daily visits to the Blessed Sacrament. And he prayed to the good Lord that many others would think about and love these suffering souls.

Several times a day John sprinkled holy water on the ground, a practice he insisted was a great help to these unseen sufferers. He also offered hundreds of short aspirations throughout the day. Then there was the highest act of prayer, the Holy Mass, during which he begged the good God to grant eternal rest to all sufferers. When anyone came to him asking prayers for an urgent need, he would recommend a *novena of Masses* as most efficacious.

This charity and zeal for the souls in purgatory were so pleasing to God, that he permitted multitudes of souls to appear to John. Once a vast throng of souls, like doves soaring heavenward, came to him expressing thanks for their liberation, while at the same time a host of others appeared languishing in agony. Often during the night, he would hear pitiful cries: "Friar John, how long must we remain in so much suffering? Pray for me... for me... for me! I have greater need!" These cries of woe distressed the saint and moved him to redouble his prayers and sprinkle more holy water.

We can learn and remember great lessons from our "purgatory saint." Holy water is a powerful sacramental to aid the holy souls, as well as indulgences, prayers, and visits to the Blessed Sacrament.

(Alongside the Mass, the Holy Rosary is the most powerful and richly indulgenced devotion in relieving the suffering souls in purgatory. When we pray the Rosary, we have a powerhouse of grace so potent that it explodes open the gates of purgatory. The Rosary is more powerful than an atomic bomb. It is more powerful than a thousand suns! And it is ours.)

At sixty years old, St. John Macias closed his eyes to the world on September 16, 1645. He is buried at the Church of St. Dominic in Lima, Peru.

That prayers and penances for the faithful departed are pleasing and acceptable to God we know by John's confession on his deathbed. St. John Macias' friend, St. John the Evangelist, revealed to him that his prayers had liberated more than 1.4 million souls from their confinement. On his deathbed, it was said, the heavens opened and those souls rushed down to escort him to heaven. What a welcome!

Make this the best year for "souls rescue!" Happy is he who lays up for himself the support of his brothers and sisters in heaven for the day of his own departure from earth.

By delivering the souls in purgatory, by hastening their entrances into heaven, we draw to ourselves the gratitude of all paradise and forge bonds of friendship with all its inhabitants.

St. John Macias, pray for us!

St. Padre Pio Helped Purgatorial Souls

"More souls of the dead from purgatory than of the living climb this mountain to attend my Masses and seek my prayers."

— St. Pio of Pietrelcina

As with all the great saints, "Padre Pio," the famed twentieth-century Franciscan stigmatic from Italy, had a special relationship with the holy souls. They were his frequent visitors, to such an extent that he once said, "I see so many souls from purgatory, they don't frighten me anymore." In fact, St. Pio once related that he encountered more souls from purgatory than he did those who were still in this world!

Padre Pio received souls, including those of deceased soldiers during World War II who, it was said, lined up for his intercession. In one case, a monk who lived with him spotted strange soldiers near the friary's fireplace. Wondering how they got in, Padre Pio explained that they were not actual soldiers but departed spirits who had stopped by for help on their way to the hereafter.

A great saint this was! Such souls beseeched him constantly, and he offered his powerful two-hour Masses along with personal sufferings for their release. He knew the importance, and the power, of supplication. He also knew the power of suffering. He knew that all that matters is doing God's will and fulfilling your duty according to your state in life. He knew that the key to God's heart is prayer, and that the Rosary is one of the best "weapons" we have.

One truly enlightening story is important to know. A doctor who was very close to Padre Pio received a letter from a woman whose daughter was near death. The mother implored the future saint for his priestly prayers and blessings. The doctor was unable to get this letter to Padre Pio until several days after he had received it. After reading the letter to Padre Pio, this physician asked how should he answer it. Pio responded, "Fiat."

The doctor knew that some time had passed since he had received the letter, and that the girl was at death's door. He was perplexed by Padre Pio's assurance that all was done, that the request for prayer would work. The Capuchin priest continued, "Maybe you don't know that I can pray even now for the happy death of my great-grandfather." "But he has been dead for many, many years," replied the doctor. "I know that too," said Padre Pio. "Let me explain by giving you an example.

"You and I both die and through the good fortune and the goodness and mercy of the Lord we are obliged to stay in purgatory for 100 years. During these years nobody prays for us or has a Mass offered for the release of our souls. The 100 years pass and somebody thinks of Padre Pio and the good doctor and has Masses offered. For Our Lord, the past does not exist; the future does not exist. Everything is an eternal present. Those prayers had already been taken into account so that even now I can pray for the happy death of my great-grandfather! Do you really think the Lord needs our bureaucracy — that somebody has to ask for a grace on a piece of paper and bring it to Padre Pio?"

The important lesson is that we should always pray for the deceased, even those who have died many years ago, because for God there is neither a past nor a future, but all as one eternal present.

Let us join together with the holy souls in shouting as they were heard to do on one occasion in the friary of San Giovanni Rotondo: *"Viva Padre Pio!"* (Long live Padre Pio!)

The little girl in need of prayer, by the way, was healed.

St. Philip Neri and the "Purgatory Box"

"As you did it to one of the least of these my brethren, you did it to me."

— MATTHEW 25:40

Born in Florence, Italy, in 1515, St. Philip Neri, one of the most memorable of those raised to the altar, came from a poor family and was influenced by Dominicans. He preached on the street corners of Rome to whoever would listen. He is known as the "Apostle of Rome" for his evangelization. But the point is: This saint was vibrant with the most tender love for the poor souls in purgatory.

He prayed constantly for them, and bestowed on them the merits of his good works. St. Philip taught his oratorians to pray and do redemptive suffering for the poor souls. He was particularly anxious to help those souls who during life had been under his spiritual care. He considered he owed more to them because, as a priest, he had labored for the salvation of their souls. He was often made aware of their release.

Many dead appeared to Father Philip in the hope that they would be delivered through his intercession from purgatory — and indeed he never failed to pray for them. The saint was all the more anxious to pray for the dead, as they often obtained great graces for him.

After St. Philip died, a priest was praying at his tomb, and St. Philip appeared to him in radiant glory surrounded by blessed spirits. The priest asked him the meaning of the spirits. He said that these were the souls who had been under his spiritual direction during life. Having attained heaven through his intercession, they came to meet him upon his death and ushered him to the gates of paradise. They were so grateful to St. Philip for their release from purgatory, they had prayed for him until the day he died. The holy souls never forget their intercessors!

One member of St. Philip's order, the Congregation of the Oratorians, Father Magnanti, prayed unceasingly for the dead and like Father Philip was often made aware of their entry into heaven — to the point where he kept an alms box that he called the "box of the souls." Alms of the faithful were put in this box and distributed among the poor and sick. To the treasury of his alms, Father Magnanti added his Masses, fasts, and vigils. His burning love for the poor souls carried him so far that he was granted from Our Lord the sufferings of the souls in purgatory in order to give them relief.

The souls of the faithful departed were not ungrateful to him. He received numerous graces that he attributed to their intercession. He had the gift of discovering hidden sins, knowing the future, and escaping the snares of the enemy.

The devotional purgatory practice of the "box of the souls" was very common among religious orders. Consider Padre Pio. At the friary of San Giovanni Rotondo, this saint often made use of the "Purgatory Box" located on the landing in the cloister. It contained a list of one hundred sins from which souls in purgatory were being cleansed and was titled: "A Short and Easy Way to Pray for the Souls in Purgatory."

When passing by, St. Pio would select a card and recite an "Eternal Rest Prayer" for those souls being purged of the indicated sin. How important it is to always keep them in mind!

As families, we, too, could have a place in our homes for a "Purgatory Box" to remember to pray for the souls and teach our children and grandchildren to remember the souls every day. A shoe box or, perhaps, a bowl can be used. If we succeed in bringing one soul into heaven we have procured more glory to God than we could give him ourselves.

For the love of God, for the sake of Jesus, Mary, and the good St. Joseph, let us be generous to these suffering souls and remember that when we obtain their deliverance it is no ordinary alms we give them but God himself! Not a God hidden or seen from a distance, but God seen face-to-face and possessed forever.

Besides the help we procure for the souls of the departed, Jesus has promised that for every sacrifice we make, he will reward us a hundredfold in eternity. The promise of heaven is ours.

Ite ad Joseph — Go to Joseph!

"I do not remember that I ever asked St. Joseph at any time anything which he did not obtain for me."
— ST. TERESA OF ÁVILA

Why should we be dedicated to St. Joseph? St. Joseph is the foster father of our judge and savior. His power is dreaded by the devil. His death is the most singularly privileged and happiest death we could ever imagine, as he died in the presence and care of Jesus and Mary. St. Joseph will obtain for us that same privilege at our passage from this life to eternity.

We are called to pray for a happy death (to die in the state of grace) for ourselves and our families and for those now near death. It is the greatest and last blessing of God in this life. We must petition God for this grace. Blessed Louis Guanella said, "There is need of living well, but there is even more need of dying well. A good death is everything." Every day over 152,000 persons die worldwide and are judged. More people are dying at a faster rate than ever before. Each time we pick up the paper or watch the news there is a crisis of huge proportion. Is it a wake-up call?

We are called through our prayers and sacrifices to assist these souls. If by your prayers, suffering, and other good works, you have obtained a good death for a dying sinner, you should look upon yourself as a mother or father to that soul.

Their souls may be on the wrong road. By your prayers you could give them the grace of repentance. You will have placed their soul in purgatory. Now you can assist by all the means possible in obtaining the soul's release from purgatory. Save the dying if you have been a stumbling block to the living.

Go to Joseph! St. Joseph repays us generously if we come to the rescue of the suffering souls. Holy Communion offered to him for seven consecutive Sundays in honor of the holy souls is what pleases him most.

St. Joseph sanctified labor, poverty, and privations by bearing them with patience, humility, and resignation to the will of God. We have many trials in life to endure. We have need of these virtues. We need many things. Make out a list of your necessities, both material and spiritual. Write them down and go confidently to St. Joseph. Let us pray especially for all the holy souls who were dedicated to St. Joseph. It has been said that the Son of God, having the keys of paradise, has given one to his Immaculate Mother and the other to St. Joseph.

To honor the heavenly Father, you honor Jesus. To honor Jesus, you honor his mother. To honor his mother, you honor Joseph. As you know, our world is in great peril. We desperately need Joseph. Are you ready to join St. Joseph in prayer?

The time has come that St. Joseph be hidden no longer. The time has come that St. Joseph be better known to the people of God. The time has come that St. Joseph receive the honor that will glorify God and bring back the most abundant blessings upon the entire world.

Lent, Fasting, and "All Souls Saturdays"

"If, each year, we are faithful in sharing Christ's sufferings during Lent and Holy Week, each year, too, the celebration of Easter, the contemplation of the glory of Jesus triumphant over death, makes us participate more fruitfully and more abundantly in the state of the risen Lord."

— Blessed Columba Marmion

One of the most revered traditions of our Roman Church, which is equally observed in the Eastern Church, is the commemoration of the departed. It is the constant teaching of the Church since apostolic times that our prayers, offerings, and good works can help departed souls.

The Eastern Catholic Church does not celebrate All Souls Day on November 2 but instead celebrates five "All Souls Saturdays," when the Eastern Church remembers their departed on Saturdays, commemorating them with the Divine Liturgy for the souls of all departed loved ones. All Souls Saturdays are given over to the souls in purgatory during the Great Lent.

The faithful submit the names of all their immediate families and friends. These names are put in a book called "The Scroll of the Departed." At the end of the Divine Liturgy all submitted names are read out loud. No one is left out, no matter how long it takes to recite them.

The book is placed in a corner where a sacred ion is located. Parishioners can venerate and pray at this icon corner during Lent. There are five All Souls Saturdays, with the first before Lent, three during Lent, and the fifth on the Saturday evening before Pentecost Sunday.

St. John Chrysostom spoke of prayer as light in the house of one's heart. He encouraged people to decorate their homes with the justice of fasting and the gold of almsgiving so that they might become perfect dwelling places for the Lord.

We also have this great power and privilege given to us to expiate for sins by enduring suffering and imitating Our Lord. Fasting is a great help to avoid sin and all that leads to it. As Pope Benedict XVI reminds us: "The practice of fasting was very present in the first Christian community (cf. Acts 13:3; 14:23; 27:21; 2 Cor 6:5). The Church Fathers, too, speak of the force of fasting to bridle sin, especially the lusts of the 'old Adam,' and open in the heart of the believer a path to God."

Moreover, fasting is a practice that is encountered frequently and recommended by the saints of every age. St. Peter Chrysologus writes: "Fasting is the soul of prayer, mercy the lifeblood of fasting. So if you pray, fast; if you fast, show mercy; if you want your petition to be heard, hear the petition of others. If you do not close your ear to others, you open God's ear to yourself" (*Sermon* 43: PL 52, 320. 322).

When we imitate Our Lord by fasting, praying, and persevering, we are able to bring our soul and all other souls we love into the sweet smelling grace of Our Lord's mercy and forgiveness which is the great goal of Lent.

Let us join our Byzantine brothers and sisters during the holy Season of Lent and let the souls of our loved ones join in the resurrection of Jesus into paradise, and mercy and forgiveness shall be ours when we meet our good God.

At the Cross with Our Lady

"Our Lady has one eye turned to God, the other to sinners.... How she comes to our aid in our needs!"
— St. Thomas of Villanova

Mary stood by when her son died for the redemption of souls. Through her whole life she had constantly before her mind the work he had come to accomplish. Now she sees those souls covered with the divine blood by which they were purchased.

The love of her Immaculate Heart embraces those in purgatory. She is the loving mother of the souls in purgatory. She, too, has gone through a fire of tribulation by which she is known as the "comforter of the afflicted." Her life was a sea of sorrow, poverty, exile, persecution, and in the separation from Jesus on the cross. All these sufferings were a real purgatory for her.

Our Lady loves the poor souls in purgatory. And like the tragic separation from her son on the cross, for a short time she has lost these souls to purgatory, which she sees separated from heaven, from her son, and from herself, and languishing in purgatory. She burns with love for the poor souls, remembering the words of her son when he said that even a cup of water in his name would be rewarded with the joy of heaven. These souls thirst desperately for God. Our Lady is their helper and comforter.

Father Père Lamy (d. 1931), a priest who was once of the same diocese as the Curé d'Ars, writes: "The Blessed Virgin hates purgatory. It is a sorry place. I love very much to pray for the souls in purgatory. The Blessed Virgin thought I did not ask enough for them. She says, 'I am pouring graces upon those souls' (graces that I did not dare ask for)."

Let us, therefore, venerate Mary and beg of her to increase our fervor and give us perseverance in good works, in receiving the sacraments worthily, in Sundays kept holy, in charity given, to obtain for us a happy death and avoid purgatory. In the words of St. Gabriel Possenti: "Don't you know what good the Blessed Virgin can do for you? She can make you a saint."

The best means to obtain this grace is to imitate the love of the Blessed Virgin for the poor souls. In the recitation of the Holy Rosary we have a spiritual bouquet of roses, which we can often offer to her for our departed loved ones. A scriptural Rosary is even more powerful because Scripture is our foundation. By meditating upon a particular passage from the Bible on each bead, a scriptural Rosary becomes the living Word of God.

A beautiful legend says that when Jesus was bleeding to death on the cross, an angel asked him to whom the last drop of his heart's blood should belong, and he answered, "To my beloved mother, that she may the more easily endure her sorrow."

"Not so, my Son," Mary is said to have answered. "Grant it to the souls in purgatory, that they may be free from pain on at least one day of the year."

In 1995 I went on a pilgrimage to Lourdes, France. As you enter this Marian shrine, a huge statue of Our Lady of Lourdes greets you. The tour guide pointed up to the statue to show us the rosary on Our Lady's arm. Our Lady had a six-decade rosary versus the traditional five-decade rosary. The tour guide said that St. Bernadette asked Our Lady what the sixth decade was for. Our Lady replied: "The sixth decade is for the souls in purgatory!"

Let us scatter these spiritual roses abundantly over the graves of our parents, children, and friends throughout the year. Mary, the mother of the poor souls, will find them fragrant, and not only accept our offering of her beloved Rosary, but also protect and guard us when our turn comes to die.

At the Root of Divine Mercy with St. Faustina

"Jesus has a remedy for everything."
— St. Faustina Kowalska

St. Maria Faustina Kowalska is known today as the "Apostle of Mercy." She was consigned the great mission by Our Lord Jesus to proclaim his message of mercy to the whole world by her example, suffering, and obedience, and by recording everything in a diary. Our Lord requested the feast of Divine Mercy be celebrated on the Second Sunday of Easter.

Jesus told St. Faustina: "On that day the very depths of My tender mercy are open. I pour out a whole ocean of graces upon souls who approach the fount of My mercy. The soul that will go to Confession, and receive Holy Communion shall obtain complete forgiveness of sins and punishment. On that day, all the divine floodgates through which graces flow are opened" (*Diary*, 699).

St. Faustina was known to be a saint of mercy for the souls in purgatory. One night she was visited by the soul of a fellow religious sister who had recently passed away. In her diary she described the poor soul as being "in a terrible condition… her face painfully distorted." In response, she redoubled her prayers for the sister's soul.

Sometime later, the soul of the sister again visited St. Faustina during the night. Her face was now "radiant, her eyes beaming with joy." She said that Faustina "had a true love for her neighbor and that many other souls had profited from her prayers." Before the soul left, she urged St. Faustina "not to cease praying for the souls in purgatory" (*Diary*, 58).

This is but one moving example of St. Faustina's great love for the holy souls in purgatory, who yearn to be united with God in heaven. Let us follow her way!

Whenever possible, St. Faustina would pray for the release of the holy souls in purgatory. During her annual retreat on January 10, 1934, she recorded Jesus' expressed desire (she heard and saw him) that she use her time in saying "short indulgenced prayers for the souls in purgatory" (*Diary*, 274). Jesus himself asked her to devote the eighth day of the Divine Mercy Novena to praying for the release of the souls in purgatory (*Diary*, 1226).

Jesus gave St. Faustina an intense yearning for him in Holy Communion to help her understand "what the longing of the souls in purgatory" is like. On July 10, 1937, St. Faustina attended Holy Mass and experienced "such intense hunger for God" that she seemed "to be dying of the desire to be united with Jesus." She explained that only the night before, she had been fasting and offering all her spiritual exercises for one of the deceased sisters (*Diary*, 1185-86).

Such mystical literature tells us that as these souls draw closer to heaven, they begin to radiate Our Lord's joy, and indeed St. Faustina perceived this reality as she prayed for particular souls.

In the vision of purgatory, St. Faustina asks the holy souls what their "greatest suffering" is. In one voice, they answer that it is their "longing for God" (*Diary*, 20).

We, too, can be united with St. Faustina in heaven in praying for these suffering souls. The greatest loss most of us experience in this life is the death of a loved one. *The greatest desire of a soul in purgatory is to be with God.*

When St. Faustina was visited by a fellow sister in purgatory, the soul bid her to have one Mass offered for her and three ejaculatory prayers (*Diary*, 21) because Mass is the greatest means to help such souls reach God. Their ticket to heaven is in the Holy Sacrifice!

The founder of the Marians of the Immaculate Conception, Blessed Stanislaus Papczynski, who lived in Poland in the seventeenth century and whose order led the way for the canonization of St. Faustina, felt a special duty to help purgatorial souls. They were obliged to pray the entire Rosary and the Office for the Dead every day.

The idea of helping souls was the result of both the need of the times and Father Stanislaus' deep personal experiences. The never-ending wars with Moscow, the Cossacks, Turks, Tartars, and Sweden, as well as the internal turmoil, brought a rich harvest of death. Natural disasters, hunger, and epidemics increased it even more. People were dying by the thousands and so often going unprepared before God for their last judgment — very much like our time.

And so it was, in such a manner, that Christian love prompted Father Stanislaus to think about the prisoners of purgatory and rush to their aid. In his long prayers — sometimes lasting the entire night — he would allegedly descend in spirit to purgatory and stay with the souls suffering there.

During a family gathering, Father Stanislaus saw the souls suffering in purgatory, got up from the table, and in his haste to go to the chapel to pray for them, walked right through the table.

"Pray brethren, for the souls in purgatory, for they suffer unbearably," he told his confreres later. Then he locked himself in his cell for three days and prayed for those souls yet more. It is believed that many of the fallen soldiers appeared to him for help, and Father Stanislaus decided that helping the souls of the dead, especially those who perished during a war or pestilence, should be a key goal of his congregation. To this day, the second special calling for the Marian Fathers is to "offer our lives for the holy souls in purgatory, especially the victims of war and disease."

Another spiritual practice in remembrance of the holy souls in purgatory continues to this day.

The Marian Fathers "board for the holy souls" originated in the eighteenth century. Fifty different groups — or categories — of departed souls (such as parents, benefactors, popes, bishops, priests, leaders of nations, those who promoted devotion to the Immaculate Conception, and those whom God wants out of purgatory as soon as possible) are listed on a board. Every intention has a number attached to it. A number is picked from a container and matched with the intention on the board. The member of the community then offers his day of work and prayer for that group of souls. The board is located outside the chapel, and these various souls are remembered all year long.

United with St. Faustina in heaven, and following the example of Blessed Stanislaus, let us boldly ask the Father of Mercies to empty purgatory! (To join with the Marian Helpers and become a member of the Holy Souls Sodality, visit their website at *www .marian.org/holysouls*.)

Let us pray as St. Faustina prayed on the eighth day of the Divine Mercy Novena: "Eternal Father... look upon the souls in purgatory in no other way than through the wounds of Jesus,

Your dearly beloved Son; for we firmly believe that there is no limit to Your goodness and compassion" (*Diary*, 1227).

St. Catherine of Genoa:
The "Apostle of Purgatory"

"You cannot see my face; for man shall not see me and live."
— EXODUS 33:20

St. Catherine of Genoa (d. 1510), mystic and laywoman, is also known as the "Apostle of Purgatory" and the most authoritative saint on this subject.

Her treatise on purgatory explores the attitude of the holy souls, what they suffer, why they suffer, why they willingly choose to go there, the consolations of those souls, and how — by expiating our sins in this life — we can shorten or avoid pain after.

St. Catherine said that he who purifies from faults in this present life satisfies with a penny a debt of a thousand dollars, and that he who waits until the other life to pay his debts pays the one thousand dollars instead of that penny!

St. Catherine tells us that the souls retain no knowledge of why they are in purgatory. At their judgment, they see why they are going to purgatory, but never again while they are there. "Such is their joy in God's will, in His pleasure, that they have no concern for themselves but dwell only on their joy in God's ordinance, in having Him do what He will. They see only the goodness of God, His mercy towards men. Should they be aware of other good or evil, theirs would not be perfect charity."

St. Catherine said she saw that the source of all suffering is either original sin or actual sin. She taught that God created the soul pure, simple, free from every stain, and with certain beatific instinct toward himself.

The Lord told St. Catherine that the soul is like gold, and gold is refined of its impurities, of course, by fire. St. Catherine relates, "God, who is good and great, destroys all which is of man, and purgatory purifies it."

In St. Catherine's treatise on purgatory, she writes: "Either in this life or in the life to come, the soul that seeks union with God must be purged by 'the fiery Love of God.' The holy souls are purged of all the rust and stains of sin which they have not rid themselves in this life. The fire of purgatory is first of all the fiery Love of God." Love is the basis of this process.

Purgatory is the last stage of God's love for the soul and the soul for God. She writes: "This, the last stage of love, is the pure and intense love of God alone. In this transformation, the action of God in penetrating the soul is so fierce that it seems to set the body on fire and to keep it burning until death. The overwhelming love of God gives it a joy beyond words."

The saint goes on to say that she has experienced these feelings in her own soul and can describe the joy which accompanies the pains of purgatory, and the consolation which the souls experience. "I do not believe," says the saint, "that it is possible to find a contentment to compare with that of the souls in purgatory, unless it be the contentment of the Saints in Paradise. This contentment increases daily, through the influx of God into those souls, and this influx increases in proportion as the impediment is consumed and worn away. But this contentment does not take away one bit of pain. As the soul grows in perfection, so does it suffer more because of what impedes the final consummation, the end for which God made it; so that in purgatory great joy and great suffering do not exclude one another."

She also wrote: "Were a soul to appear in the presence of God with one hour of purgation still due, it would consider itself grievously injured and its suffering would be worse than that of ten purgatories, for it could not endure the justice and pure goodness of God."

St. Catherine concludes her treatise with an appeal to the world to do penance for their sins:

> I would willingly send up a cry so loud that it would put fear in all men on the earth. I would say to them: Wretches, why do you let yourselves be thus blinded by the world, you whose need is so great and grievous (as you will know at the moment of death) and who make no provision for it whatsoever? You have all taken shelter beneath hope in God's mercy, which is, you say, very great, but you do not see that this great goodness of God will judge you for having gone against the will of so good a Lord. His goodness should compel you to do *all* His will, not give you hope in ill-doing, for His justice cannot fail, but in one way or another must be fully satisfied.

God does not wish us to have an excessive fear of purgatory. He wishes that our fear should be tempered by trust in his mercy, and that we should fear only to avoid sin at all cost and be roused to love, forgiveness, the sacramental life, and fervent prayer for the suffering souls in purgatory.

Purgatory is the glorification of God's mercy, a beautiful, powerful sign of God's love. We should be full of gratitude for this merciful doctrine. In purgatory the outrage we have committed against God's glory is really repaired by some wonderful arrangement of his merciful heart.

We can still more greatly glorify him by helping him to release these holy sufferers of his justice, so they can go to praise him and enjoy him forever in heaven.

St. Teresa of Ávila Shows How to Help by Prayer

"The pain of loss, the privation of the sight of God exceeds all the most excruciating sufferings we can imagine."
— St. Teresa of Ávila

Doctor of the Church, mystic, founder of reformed Carmelite convents, and canonized only forty-six years after her death, St. Teresa was born in Ávila, Spain, on March 28, 1515.

Formed in poverty, in suffering, in face of endless difficulties, but supported always by the mighty hand of God, is the way she summed up the story of her foundations. God visited her in visions and revelations, including information on assisting the souls in purgatory.

One example is Don Bernardine of De Mendoza, the brother of Ávila's bishop, who felt compelled by his love for the Blessed Virgin to offer St. Teresa one of his houses near a place called Valadolid for a Carmelite foundation.

Two months after his offer was accepted, Don Bernardine suddenly fell ill, could no longer speak, and was thus unable to make his confession (but gave visible proof of his sincere contrition). He died far from where St. Teresa was at the time.

"My daughter," Our Lord told her, "his salvation has been in great danger, but I have had compassion on him, and have shown him mercy, in consideration of the service which he has rendered to my mother in giving that house for the establishment of a monastery of her order. Nevertheless, he will not leave purgatory until the first Mass shall have been offered in the new convent."

What a story this is! From that day, said Teresa, the grievous sufferings of Bernardine's soul were so present to her that in spite of the great desire to build a new foundation in Toledo, she pressed forward to complete the foundation in Valadolid first. She arrived there on the feast of St. Lawrence, arrangements were made, and the Holy Sacrifice of the Mass was offered.

At the moment of Communion, as the priest advanced toward her holding the ciborium and St. Teresa received the sacred host, Bernadine appeared to her with a shining countenance.

As the saint wrote, he "thanked me and I saw him ascend immediately to heaven. Great is the mercy of Our Lord and wonderfully acceptable is any service rendered to his Blessed Mother." We can see that our Savior takes into account the services rendered to his saints and above all, to his mother, when the soul faces him at the particular judgment.

The duration and the intensity of purgatory are affected. Thanks to the intercession of the Virgin Mary, Bernardine's purgatory was very short!

Don Bernardine's release was due to the suffrages and satisfactions offered by the faithful of the Church Militant. The angels and saints present these suffrages to God, and add to them the weight of their own merit. Their personal intervention increases the efficacy of these suffrages and augments their value in proportion to their own sanctity and glory.

In Exodus 20:5-6, God says, "I the Lord your God am a jealous God, visiting the iniquity of the fathers upon the children to the third and fourth generation of those who hate me, but showing steadfast love to thousands of those who love me and keep my commandments."

Offer Gregorian Masses or a novena of Masses for healing your family tree back to the fourth generation. Offer Masses for all ancestors back to Adam and Eve. In the horizontal relationships include brothers, sisters, cousins, uncles, aunts, step-brothers or -sisters, half-brothers or -sisters, etc. Include those not yet conceived or born. Any associates or friends who have left either a negative or positive impact on our lives should also be included, even those who have injured us or given a bad example. Remember your teachers, pastors, supervisors, and government leaders. Remember your enemies!

Those souls whose happiness has been hastened by our Masses will never forget us; they will interest themselves in our welfare and families. They become like our guardian angels. Sometimes it is a sudden inspiration to change our plans, to give up some undertaking in which our lives would have been in danger. They show that blessings and consolations of all kinds are promised in return for generous devotion to the departed.

Happy and blessed are they who pray for the dead at all seasons of the year. On earth they will have joy, confidence, and peace; and in heaven rest, happiness, and an eternal reward.

Anne Catherine Emmerich Glimpsed the Fruit of Her Intercession

"Christians, consider what an inheritance is promised you.... The Father himself shall be our inheritance!"
— St. Augustine

Blessed Anne Catherine Emmerich (d. 1824), whose revelations on the Passion of Our Lord are so well known, had a special devotion to the souls in purgatory, who often came to ask for her help.

She would kneel in the snow on winter nights and pray for them until she was stiff with cold. At other times, she would kneel on a piece of wood with sharp edges in order to increase the efficacy of her prayers by her penances; and she often had the consolation of receiving the thanks of the souls she had delivered!

She related the following story. "When I was still a child, I was led by an unknown person to a place which seemed to me to be purgatory. I saw many souls suffering grievously, who earnestly asked for my prayers. I seemed to be gazing into a deep abyss of vast extent, terrible to look upon; but it was a touching sight, for the place was full of silent persons, who seemed to be in great affliction, and yet there was something in their countenances which showed that in their hearts they had hope in the mercy of God.

"When I prayed with fervor for the poor souls, I often heard voices around me crying, 'Thank you! Thank you!' When I was older I was going early one morning to Mass, and I chose a lonely road to pray better for the souls in purgatory. It was still dark, but the poor souls that hovered above me in the air lighted my way. I was delighted to see them, for I knew them and loved them; and in the night also they used to come and ask for my assistance."

The relationship of Anne with the suffering souls was affected by the guidance of an angel who led her through the vast spaces of purgatory in order that she might be refreshed by the fruits of her penances, seeing as she was able, those who were destitute of spiritual aid.

"I was with my guide near the poor souls," she noted. "I saw their great desolation, for they cannot help themselves, and the living seem to do so little for them." Anne then continued:

While I was thinking of their misery, I was accidentally separated from my guide. I hastened to find him, searching everywhere until I was nearly fainting with terror and fatigue. I saw him at last, and he said to me, *"Now you understand something of what these poor souls must feel in their longing for help."*

My guardian angel often led me into solitary places that I might pray for the poor souls, and in tears, with arms outstretched, I implored God to have mercy on them.

Those poor souls are so grateful for all that is done for them; and when I offer my sufferings on their behalf, they pray for me in return. It frightens me to see how men neglect and despise the graces that the Church offers them in such abundance while the poor souls in purgatory languish with desire of them.

She added: "The prayer most pleasing to God is that made for others and particularly for the poor souls. Pray for them if you wish your prayers to bring high interest."

St. Margaret of Cortona: The "Mary Magdalene"
of the Seraphic Order

The Lord delivers him in the day of trouble; the Lord pro-
tects him and keeps him alive.

— Psalm 41:1-2

St. Margaret of Cortona (d. 1297) was a great sinner in her youth. She lost her mother when quite young, and so was mostly left to herself. Her beauty and lively temperament soon led her into a sinful life which lasted for a considerable time. She was swept off her feet by a handsome young lord. They lived together for many years, but the young lord would never commit to marriage. They even had a son together.

One day the lord went off to inspect his estate and was assassinated. When she found his decomposed body, Margaret realized that it symbolized the state of her soul. This led to her conversion.

Margaret left Montepuciano for her father's home in Cortona. Her father and stepmother would not welcome her or her young son. She went to the Franciscans, who gave them a place in their home and provided Margaret with spiritual direction.

Margaret became a Third Order Franciscan, and her son later became a Friar Minor. She founded a hospital, St. Mary of Mercy, still in operation today. Interestingly enough, she became known as the "Magdalene of the Seraphic Order."

After her conversion, most striking was her love and devotion for the poor souls in purgatory, for whose deliverance she sacrificed her time and rest. Not only did Margaret show compassion for the poor souls, but she always remembered her deceased mother and father, and her uncharitable stepmother, all of whom had rejected her and her son. She offered up Communions, Masses, and other good works. God revealed to her that she had very much shortened their sufferings in purgatory as a result and delivered their souls to paradise.

Margaret prayed with great ardor for all the dead, whether known or unknown to her. It was her special daily occupation. Her every thought and desire were tending toward the release of the suffering souls. This was her goal. She forgot her own self for all the merits which she gained by her virtuous and penitential life and bestowed unselfish love on her poor suffering souls.

St. Margaret also did all in her power to impart this devotion to others, especially to priests and nuns.

Our Lord told her to recommend the poor souls to the Friars Minor of St. Francis, saying: "Recommend them, in my name, to think of the poor souls, whose number, at the present moment, is innumerable, because there are scarcely any people who pray for them."

Great was St. Margaret's reward for it! As she lay on her deathbed, she saw a crowd of souls — released by her suffrages — hastening to her side to form, as it were, a guard of honor escorting her to eternity.

If we earnestly pray, we shall find prayers; if we offer our suffrages, we shall find them; if we free others, we ourselves shall be freed.

Those who practice charity will receive charity. Those who are merciful will receive mercy. Whoever frees a soul from purgatory will find a host of friendly souls surrounding his or her deathbed.

The Role of Guardian Angels on Earth and in Purgatory

"The Lord has sent his angel and rescued me."
— Acts 12:11

From the time of our birth, God has graced us with a faithful companion, appointed guardian and guide: our dear guardian angel. Angels are spiritual beings who are constantly in God's presence, singing praises to our Creator. Angels serve as divine messengers, bringing God's will and word to all humanity. Although we are unable to see them, they are there, ready to protect and watch over us at God's command.

The Doctors of the Church teach that the guardianship of the holy angels over men only terminates at the souls' entrance into heaven. If we heed the Church and invoke our guardian angels throughout life they will be a most powerful help for us at the hour of death, strengthening us against temptation and comforting us in our agony.

They conduct our souls to judgment. We are assured the angels console us if we are in purgatory, encourage us, and render a most valuable service by inspiring friends and relatives to offer a holy Mass for our intentions and practice good works for our speedy delivery.

These devoted guardians, to whom we should pray each day, asking their help in purifying us here on earth, never cease to be concerned with the souls that God has committed to their charge. Their great mission and desire is to see us home in heaven. They are intent on obtaining from God all the graces and favors conducive to our eternal welfare.

The guardian angels pray for their charges with great love before the throne of God and ascend to present their petitions in our favor. They descend to bring to the souls in purgatory the favors which they obtained for them from God through the good works of the faithful on earth and, it is said, pass by our place in heaven every day.

The guardian angels inform the souls in purgatory who their benefactors are and exhort them to pray for those who help them. As St. Augustine said: "The departed may be informed by the angels of things happening in this world, in so far as this is permitted by Him to whose judgment everything is subject." The souls cannot pray for themselves but can pray and intercede for us while they are in purgatory and then in heaven.

As St. Margaret of Cortona was praying to Our Lord with tears for all the friends she had lost, they appeared to her surrounded by purifying flames and in such lamentable condition that she could not endure the sight. Our divine Redeemer said to her: "The pains they endure are very great, but would be incomparably greater if they were not visited and consoled by my angels, the sight of whom comforts them in their sufferings and refreshes in their purification."

St. Jerome expressed: "How great the dignity of the soul, since each one has from birth an angel commissioned to guard it." Throughout your life give alms and offer Masses for your living and deceased loved ones and friends in the name of your guardian angel. Light a candle in honor of him.

When entering a church, unite your intention with that of your angel to adore the Blessed Sacrament. It is said the one thing the angel is unable to do that humans can do is to receive Holy Communion. Receive Holy Communion in your angel's honor. Invoke your guardian angel at the beginning of your day and in the evening making an act of loving thanksgiving.

Recite the chaplet of the guardian angel. Spend some time each day in company with your angel alone. Celebrate the feast of the guardian angels, and make your birthday a special feast of your angel who then began his ministry. Practice some devotion to the Queen of Angels in the name of your guardian angel.

The guardian angels are the natural intermediaries between earth and purgatory, as they are between purgatory and heaven. What consolation this is to those who during their lives have shown devotion! How often these souls, if they are detained in purgatory, will be visited by these pure and charitable spirits.

Our Lady of Knock's Connection to the Souls

"Mary pours her mercies on all who have recourse to her."
— St. Alphonsus Liguori

At about eight o'clock on the Thursday evening of August 21, 1879, the Blessed Virgin Mary, St. Joseph, and St. John the Evangelist appeared at the south gable of the church at Knock, County Mayo, Ireland. Beside them and a little to the right were an altar with a cross and the figure of a lamb, around which angels hovered.

There were fifteen official witnesses to the apparition, both young and old. They watched it for two hours in pouring rain and recited the Rosary. Today, Knock ranks among the world's major Marian shrines with the full approval of the Church. Pope John Paul II visited the shrine on September 30, 1979, presenting the Golden Rose (the highest honor within the Catholic Church) to this shrine.

Not everyone is aware, however, that the marvelous appearance on the gable of the Knock church came on the day when the parish priest, Father Bartholomew Cavanagh, finished offering, as he had promised, one hundred Masses for the suffering souls in purgatory! A few months before the apparition the pastor began to offer one hundred Masses for the poor souls whom Our Lady wished most to release. It was on the day the one hundredth Mass was offered that Our Lady came to visit Knock.

Surely, that extraordinary devotion to the holy souls had a part to play in the gift of the vision from heaven. If such a response came from heaven to Father Cavanagh, then certainly Our Lady wants to encourage us all to remove the torment of our dead. Our Lady is the mother of her children, above all her suffering children. She is the Refuge of Sinners on earth and in purgatory.

Indeed, we can dig deeper there for a link with our own day regarding this apparition. The *reason* the parish priest turned in this way to the holy souls was because of a painful problem similar to what affects many countries today. A secret organization resorting to violence had threatened the priest by letter for preaching against their tactics. They resented his condemnation of violence, which prevented them from gaining recruits in the Knock parish. In his distress, he turned to the suffering souls and called on his parishioners to fill the church for one hundred days of these offered Masses. And what an answer he was given from heaven!

The holy souls stopped the violence through Our Lady's intercession at Knock. This applies to our day with the horrific violence and terrorist attacks around the world. Now is the time to act!

Here are some powerful means to help: Ask a priest, perhaps one who is retired, to say one hundred Masses for the holy souls for the intention of world peace. This has been done in some major cities. Attend Mass and receive Holy Communion on those days. If that is not possible, you yourself can offer one hundred Masses for the souls in purgatory on behalf of world peace and ask others to do the same during those days.

We lay up treasure of which God will give us the benefit in the days of trial. We are ensuring a favorable welcome for our own soul when our last hour draws near. Who is like God? No one is as good as God, whose mercy is unfathomable and infinite. Therefore, our divine Savior will do much more for us than we have done for the faithful departed.

He who is goodness and mercy itself will open for us his treasures and make us partakers of his infinite merits, and the debt we owe will be paid to the last penny. *Nothing will delay our entrance into heaven.*

Father Cavanagh is buried on the grounds of the Knock shrine. The altar where the one hundred Masses were offered still exists and is located in the chapel. Mass continues to be offered on that sacred altar to this day.

Our Lady of Knock, pray for us!

Purgatory Island Teaches Secrets of Helping Souls

"Is not this the fast that I choose: to loose the bonds of wickedness, to undo the thongs of the yoke, to let the oppressed go free, and to break every yoke?"

— ISAIAH 58:6-7

Station Island in Lough Derg, County Donegal, Ireland, is an ancient pilgrimage place called St. Patrick's Purgatory. Here we really learn about penance and helping the cherished souls!

Legend has it that St. Patrick stayed in a cave here, where he had visions of heaven, hell, and purgatory. Annually, for more than a thousand years, from June 1 to August 15 pilgrims have fasted for three days and walked barefoot repeating designated station prayers on the island and doing a bit of "purgatory" here on earth: staying up all night, fasting, praying with rare intensity, and helping those who have gone before us.

Spiritual exercises are also performed in the names of seven saints associated with each of the penitential beds or stations: St. Brigid, St. Brendan, St. Catherine, St. Columba, St. Patrick, St. Davog, and St. Molaise.

These beds on Station Island are remains of rings of boulders of monastic cells or oratories where the monks spent time alone in prayer.

This pilgrimage is a journey of conversion of the heart and a place to offer suffrages for the souls in purgatory. Devotions include familiar prayers of petition and thanksgiving, daily Mass, the Rosary, the Way of the Cross, renewal of baptismal vows, and benediction. Fasting is an integral part of this tradition. A Lough Derg meal is permitted once a day, consisting of black tea or coffee and dry bread, toast, or oatcakes.

Scripture reveals to us that prayer and fasting has been practiced since the time of Our Lord and throughout the ages by all the great saints. In the Old Testament, people fasted to ask forgiveness, seek health, and assist the dead. Fasting goes beyond the realm of food and into our actions and thoughts.

We allow God to use fasting to move us forward on our way to holiness. It purifies our hearts in order to open them wide to God and to the spiritual and temporal needs of our neighbors. True fasting is linked with almsgiving and prayer.

The archangel Raphael deserves credit when he tells us that it is better to give alms than to lay up treasures of gold because that purges away every sin and delivers us from death.

After an all-night vigil, toast and tea, and the penance of staying awake, the sacrament of reconciliation and the celebration of Holy Mass take on a more intense experience. Tea and toast are replaced with the true bread of life and cup of eternal salvation.

Since the fifth century, pilgrims have visited Purgatory Island to cleanse their souls and reconcile themselves with God and neighbor. Many of us are unable to visit St. Patrick's Purgatory, but we can create our own Purgatory Island to lend our helping hands in lifting souls out of the purgatorial pit as we have the power and privilege to do so.

Let us not permit so many days to pass and so many occasions to slip out of our hands without relieving or releasing souls in purgatory, when we can do it with so much ease. St. Patrick, Our Lady, and the pastor at Knock — Father Cavanagh — would be proud of us. So would Our Lord.

Extraordinary Benefits and Consolation of Prayer

"The measure you give will be the measure you get back."
— LUKE 6:38

What would you wish for if you were in purgatory? Not to be forgotten, to be remembered by your loved ones and friends in the prayers offered in the Holy Sacrifice of the Mass. Even the greatest saints begged to be remembered in our prayers.

The Venerable Sister Paula of St. Teresa (d. 1657) was a Dominican nun of the convent of St. Catherine of Siena in Naples, Italy. One day while praying she was transported in spirit to purgatory where she saw a great number of souls languishing patiently, detained from God.

Close to them she saw Our Lord, attended by his angels who pointed out, one after the other, several souls that he desired to take to heaven, whereupon they ascended there. At this sight, the servant of God, addressing herself to her divine spouse, said to him: "O my beloved Lord, why this choice among such a vast multitude?"

He replied, "I have released those who during life performed great acts of charity and mercy, and who have merited that I should fulfill my promise in their regard, 'Blessed are the merciful, for they shall obtain mercy'" (Mt 5:7). The lesson? We will find compassion in the afterlife in the proportion we have acted mercifully in this life.

When we work for the souls in purgatory, we work for ourselves. We should have much confidence in these holy souls. God hears their pleas, for their prayers possess all the qualities pleasing to him: a living faith, ardent charity, and purity of intentions. They know of us by their own experience: the trials, temptations, and struggles we face. They know better than we do the efficacy and necessity of divine grace. All the more are they impelled to become our intercessors.

The Venerable Frances of the Blessed Sacrament (d. 1629) assures us that the holy souls assisted her in all dangers and disclosed to her the snares of the devil. A soul appearing to her said: "Fear not, we will always defend you." Another soul assured her, "We pray daily for you; and as often as anyone remembers us, we also remember him and intercede for him with God. Especially do we implore for him the grace to serve God well and to die a happy death."

Do we not all want (and need) such help? By devotion to the holy souls, our progress in virtue and perfection is greatly hastened.

St. Gregory the Great said that there are thousands of instances from which we may learn how efficiently the holy souls can obtain for us health in sickness, aid in poverty, relief in distress, counsel in doubt, and protection in danger. The more souls you release from purgatory, the more protectors you will have in heaven, where they will continually implore God for your welfare.

What a consolation to know at the hour of death that we will have escorts to heaven!

The renowned historian Cardinal Cesare Baronius (d. 1607) relates: A man of great virtue was at the hour of his death. He was battered by evil spirits. Suddenly he saw the heavens open and thousands of warriors in white garments coming to his aid. They told him that they were sent to defend him and to gain victory for him. The dying man was greatly relieved and asked his heavenly defenders who they were. They replied: "We are the souls whom you released. We come to reward your charity, and to conduct your soul to heaven." After receiving this assurance, he died.

Now, in our own day, in 1997, a woman from Australia named Muriel started up with a group of seven people the practice of offering up one day a week for the holy souls. Muriel became ill and was dying. As she lay on her deathbed, she was a little afraid. Suddenly, there were hundreds of people walking past her bed. The crowds were coming out of the woods!

She asked, "Who are you?" And a voice replied, "They are your holy souls, Muriel. They have come to thank you." The holy souls nodded at her acknowledgment. They wanted her to keep praying for them and not to forget them. They still needed her prayers.

Muriel did not know any of the souls. She was surprised at that. There seemed to her to be hundreds of soldiers from the trenches of the First World War. There was a bride and groom together. All types of people from all walks of life. Some were from many years ago in olden-day dress, and some were more recent. As they passed, nodding at her, they vanished.

Muriel understood that her prayers, Masses, and sacrifices were greatly appreciated by them, and it gave her confidence that when she would die, they would be there for her. She was no longer afraid. It was very beautiful and comforting!

A little later Muriel died a holy death after receiving the anointing of the sick and saying the joyful mysteries of the Rosary with a priest at her bedside. Her son was praying the Rosary and Litany of Our Lady. During the litany, Muriel quietly slipped from this world into the next, wearing her scapular and clutching her rosary beads.

The nurse at the hospice said it was the most beautiful death he had ever seen. The souls always remember their friends!

What a splendid sight: members of the Church Militant hold out their hands to the Church Suffering to enjoin them with the Church Triumphant. Nothing is done by itself.

Imagine the welcome the souls we release from purgatory will give to us when we enter the gates of heaven. Talk about gratitude!

Our Lady of Montligeon Leads World Center of Prayer for the Dead

"Let us ask the Blessed Virgin every day to obtain for us, through her powerful intercession, a real spirit of prayer and the gift of perseverance in prayer to the end of our days."
— ST. CHARLES OF MOUNT ARGUS

Father Paul-Joseph Buguet was born on March 25, 1843, in Bellavilliers, Orne, France. His impoverished parents could barely support young Paul and his brother, yet God graced them. Paul entered the seminary in Sees and devoted himself to God, the Church, and souls. He felt that mortification, humility, and cultivation of the inner spirit were the three things necessary to become a holy priest. Who could disagree? Paul was ordained on May 26, 1866.

Ten years later on the evening of November 1, 1876, his brother, Auguste Buguet, was ringing the bells at the Church of Our Lady of Mortagne-au-Perche, in Normandy when, incredibly, one of the bells broke loose and killed him.

Father Paul was heartsick, and only God's goodness sustained the priest. Not knowing the state of his brother's soul, he begged reassurance of God's love and mercy that his soul was saved. He abandoned himself and his brother to the will of God with confidence that not even a hair on one's head falls without the permission of the divine will. The Lord cannot want or permit anything unless it is for our good.

Father Paul prayed for his brother's soul so as to obtain his entrance into paradise. From this personal experience the priest considered this a call from heaven to commit himself to a work of mercy for the dead.

The 700-member parish of LaChapelle-Montligeon, to which Father Paul was assigned, was extremely poor. Factories were replacing old cottage-weaving industries. Machines were being invented that were replacing handmade crafts. The young were forced to go to the city for jobs. Employment was sinking, similar to today. Father Buguet wanted to give the people work without leaving their region so as to have a future for the parish and the next generation.

Father Buguet had two goals: "To have prayers offered for the neglected souls of purgatory, to free them from their pains by the Mass, which contains the supreme expiation; and in return, to obtain the means to support the worker to make a decent living. This was in my mind a reciprocal gift between the suffering souls in purgatory and the poor abandoned ones on earth. It was a mutual deliverance."

Each Monday, Mass for the deliverance of the most forgotten soul in purgatory was offered in an oratory dedicated to "St. Joseph,

Patron of a Good Death." Here an extraordinary happening took place. A woman appearing in church, wearing a sky blue dress and with her head covered by a long white veil, came to Father Buguet and asked him to celebrate a Mass for her intentions. He had never seen her before.

She came twice more and disappeared suddenly. Father Buguet confided to his closest friends that the mysterious lady praised him and thanked him "for this charity of offering Mass each Monday for the most abandoned soul in purgatory."

From this visit from Our Lady, the priest drew up the rules of "The Work of Expiation":

> My God, give me the grace to penetrate well this thought: Expiation. Ah! If I understood well all the gentleness that is in this word, I would not have the fear of mortification that I do. I would love penance, and it would be a consolation for me. Well! To diminish purgatory, do penance. For that, one can offer everything from dusk to dawn, all one's afflictions, sorrows, worries.

This "Purgatory Father" became "the traveling salesman of the souls in purgatory."

In 1887, a printing apostolate was formed to publish magazines about the work for the poor souls. Pilgrimages from other regions were organized to pray to Our Lady of Montligeon in the parish church.

A new church was raised where requests "from the entire universe will be united every day, rising together to God." A magnificent statue of Our Lady of Deliverance, designed by Father Buguet, was made for the church.

Today, Our Lady of Montligeon is known as the World Center of Prayer for the Dead. There are 9 million fraternity members. You can become a member and join an Our Lady of Montligeon Prayer Group. Visit their website at *www.sanctuaire-montligeon.com*. Offer

Masses for the most neglected souls in purgatory. Start a Monday Purgatory Prayer Group.

Who are the most abandoned souls? Nonbelievers and those who have no family to pray for them; and often, priests, bishops, and consecrated religious, whom many do not think of as needing prayers. Offer a Mass for them, and look forward to meeting them someday in the upper reaches of heaven.

Worn out from his travels, Father Buguet died in Rome on June 14, 1918. His body was brought back to Montligeon on November 16, 1921, on the feast of Our Lady, the Liberator, and now rests in the crypt under the basilica.

The Saints in Action

"The saints are desirous of our company. . . . Let us long for those who long for us; let us hasten to those who are waiting for us."

— ST. BERNARD

The saints did all in their power to atone for the faults of the faithful departed. They made reparation for their own faults, satisfied their duty to the Church Suffering, loved their enemies, forgave injuries, were patient in trials, gave alms, fasted, and gained indulgences. And the saints offered up their merits for all the souls in purgatory, and beseeched Our Lady and Jesus, who have an infinite treasure, to apply their precious merits to these saintly sufferers.

The saints shared with us a path to God, a path that leads us to helping release the suffering souls in purgatory. A path that leads to eternal life.

PART III
Apostles of Purgatory: Devotions and Practices Throughout the Year

"In our prayers, let us not forget sinners and the poor souls in purgatory, especially our poor relatives."

— St. Bernadette

The souls in purgatory are silent voices that beg and implore our help. They suffer day and night 24/7, 365 days a year, without any relief. They are forever crying out to the living, "Have mercy on us for we are lonely and poor."

We urgently need "Apostles of Purgatory" or, if you will, "Purgatory Busters" to speak of them, pray for them, and plead their cause. Be their liberators! We have a unique opportunity to be their voices and echo their cries. If we could see the power of our sacrifices and the Masses offered for the holy souls, we would devote ourselves with such earnestness that the whole world would raise their eyes and take notice and would believe.

What have we learned from the purgatory saints? We know there is a profound communion between the living and the dead. We know there are no borders between us and those who have gone before us. We know the power and great efficacy of our intercessory prayers. We know the path. Are we ready to begin the journey?

The saints' journeys are tied together to assist us with a devotion full of fervor and zeal for the holy souls in purgatory — a fervor to be passed on to all future generations, to fulfill our duty as Christians, to honor the memory of our dead, to offer prayers and suffrages for them, and to become holy as the saints are holy.

Special devotional prayers and practices for the various seasons of the year will give you the opportunity to imitate the saints and the charity of God. Reflecting on the deceased every day as a perpetual remembrance brings relief for those beloved souls in purgatory. The fruit of purgatory is purification. The remembrance of purgatorial souls will spurn us to avoid sin at all cost; and we will bring glory to God, for heaven will be opened to a multitude of souls.

So it is from us alone that the holy souls in purgatory expect relief, help, and the termination of their sufferings. WE ARE THEIR ONLY RESOURCE. We alone are their deliverers; for we alone can suffer with merit and release them. Heaven encourages them; we deliver them.

Our purgatory mission has just begun. The great Pope John Paul II emphasized that the laity will be "missionaries" because contemporary man hears witnesses more easily than teachers. He exclaimed, "You will be able to set the world on fire! The hour of the laity has struck!" (November 26, 2000, Jubilee of the Apostolate of the Laity).

When the Saints Go Marching In, We Want to Be in That Number

For two years, a friend of mine drove past a very small cemetery on her way to volunteer at a local hospital. The cemetery had no name, no fence, and approximately twenty-five headstones. Each time she passed it, she prayed for the souls in purgatory, while making the Sign of the Cross.

One day, while she was passing the cemetery on her way back home, she silently wondered if any souls were released from purgatory. She stopped for a red light, and she noticed the license plate in front of her. It read:

CU-N-HVN

That is: See You in Heaven!

It was such a euphoric feeling knowing she had released souls! And that is what's in it for you: heaven. See you there!

––––––

My previous books are great resources and contain the recommended novenas, prayers, litanies, and devotions that are listed with the seasons that follow. I call these books the pillars of prayer for the holy souls in purgatory. They include:

- *The Way of the Cross for the Holy Souls in Purgatory*
- *Praying in the Presence of Our Lord for the Holy Souls*

- *The Rosary for the Holy Souls in Purgatory*
- *Thirty-Day Devotions for the Holy Souls*
- *Prayers for Eternal Life*

A novena consists of acts of devotions performed on nine consecutive days to obtain a particular grace of either spiritual or temporal nature. Novenas also prepare the faithful for the great feasts of Our Lord, the Blessed Mother, and particular saints.

Another devotion, the litany, is a form of intense prayer imploring God, Mary, and the saints to come to our aid. They are used as prayers of intercession, for peace, pardon, and protection against calamities. They are very powerful. When Our Lady appeared at Fátima and Lourdes, she always asked the people to form processions, and litanies were prayed in her honor. They are an effective means of obtaining spiritual strength and physical assistance, too.

Choose a number of prayers and devotions. Time is of the essence. Use them.

WINTER DEVOTIONS AND SPIRITUAL PRACTICES (JANUARY/FEBRUARY/MARCH)

- Start the new year off with the First Friday and First Saturday devotions. For the practice of the Nine First Fridays devotion, Our Lord promises the grace of final repentance. For the practice of the Five First Saturdays devotion, Our Lady promises to assist at the hour of death with the graces necessary for salvation. Our Lord told Sister Lucia at Fátima not to make this devotion just once but to repeat it over and over again because it is necessary for the coming of the era of peace in the world. The Internet has detailed information about these devotions.
- Mark your calendar throughout the year for special dates as a reminder to pray for your dearly departed loved ones.

- Offer Masses year-round for living and deceased family and friends. Send to your local missions office or favorite missionary order.

- Create a family tree and offer Gregorian Masses for your parents, grandparents, etc., to the fourth generation. This is very potent and brings many graces. Offer a novena of Masses (three or nine days of Masses) for horizontal relationships for both the living and the deceased. This would include aunts, uncles, brothers, sisters, cousins, in-laws, nieces, and nephews.

- Arrange for your will to specify that Gregorian Masses be said for you. Contact the author at Our Sunday Visitor for more information.

- Pray for fifteen minutes before and after Mass in thanksgiving to Jesus and for all your ancestors who have gone before you. We would not be here if it were not for the sacrifices they made for us.

- Teach children the St. Gertrude Prayer. Include it with bedtime prayers. (See in Part II: During the Month of Souls, Recall Gertrude the Great.)

- Bring back the tradition of praying the Eternal Rest Prayer before and after meals. (See Appendix: Novena Prayers and Additional Resources.)

- Take advantage of everyday indulgences. (See in Part II: Be Greedy and Grab the Grace of Indulgences.) Review the *Handbook of Indulgences*. A calendar of indulgences is available. (See Bibliography.)

- Recite the *Te Deum*, a song of praise and thanksgiving. (This is in *Praying in the Presence of Our Lord for the Holy Souls*.)

- Pray the Litany of the Holy Name of Jesus dedicated for the month of January. (This is in *Prayers for Eternal Life*.)

- Pray the novena to Blessed Mary of Providence from January 30 to her feast day on February 7. (See Appendix: Novena Prayers and Additional Resources.)
- Pray *The Way of the Cross for the Holy Souls in Purgatory* during Lent.
- Celebrate "All Souls Saturdays" during Lent. Institute it in your parish.
- Pray the Holy Cloak Novena to St. Joseph for the holy souls in March. (Check the Internet.)
- Pray the Litany of St. Joseph dedicated for the month of March. (This is in *Prayers for Eternal Life*.)
- Become a member of the Pious Union of St. Joseph to pray for all those who will die this year. Pray the Litany of the Dying; they become the holy souls. (For more information, see *Prayers for Eternal Life*.)
- Start a purgatory prayer group or support a purgatory website. (Visit *www.marian.org/holysouls*.)
- Offer the "Heroic Act of Charity" on behalf of the holy souls, offering to God all the works of satisfaction we may gain during our lifetime and all the suffrages that may be offered for us after death. (For more information, see *Thirty-Day Devotions for the Holy Souls*.)
- Fast on Fridays in honor of Our Lord's Passion. Implement different kinds of fasting such as "fasting" from gossiping, giving in to idle curiosity, complaining, criticizing, watching TV, drinking alcohol, smoking, or other activities that give one pleasure.
- When reading the obituaries in the newspapers, pray for those who have died.
- Attend wakes and funerals to offer prayers for the family and deccased.

- Make a purgatory box or purgatory board for the family. (See in Part II: St. Philip Neri and the "Purgatory Box" and Part II: At the Root of Divine Mercy with St. Faustina.)
- Start a Dead Theologians Society chapter at your parish, high school, or college. The society inspires the youth of today to become the saints of tomorrow. Their special charism is to pray for the release of the souls in purgatory. Visit their website at *www.deadtheologianssociety.com*.
- Encourage your parish to have processions in or outside the church reciting litanies for the holy souls.

SPRING DEVOTIONS AND SPIRITUAL PRACTICES (APRIL/MAY/JUNE)

- Offer the gift of your indulgence for the holy souls at Easter and Divine Mercy Sunday (Second Sunday of Easter). Become a "Divine Mercy Apostle" by distributing prayer cards and literature inviting all to take advantage of the extraordinary Divine Mercy graces.
- Pray the Divine Mercy Novena (especially the one beginning on Good Friday) and the Chaplet of Mercy daily.
- Spread the devotion to the holy souls. Pass out books, prayer cards, and literature on the holy souls. Give this material as gifts for birthdays, anniversaries, holidays, First Holy Communion, and Confirmation. Make it available for adoration chapels, nursing homes, and prison ministry.
- At weddings, include your deceased loved ones at the petitions of the Mass.
- Plant a "prayer garden" in your yard in remembrance of the holy souls.
- Pray the Daily Novena for the Holy Souls. (This is in *Praying in the Presence of Our Lord for the Holy Souls*.)
- Pray the Chaplet of the Holy Wounds. (This is in *Praying in the Presence of Our Lord for the Holy Souls*.)

- Pray the Litany of Our Lady of Loreto dedicated for the month of May. (This is in *Prayers for Eternal Life*.)
- Pray the Litany to the Sacred Heart of Jesus dedicated for the month of June.
- Recite Psalm 130, the official prayer of the Church for the holy souls.
- When praying the Rosary in May, add an extra decade for the holy souls. Make six-decade rosaries for the holy souls and give them to your family and friends! (St. Bernadette encouraged this style of Rosary!)
- Become a member of the Fraternity of Our Lady of Montligeon. Its website is *www.sanctuaire-montligeon.com*.
- Pray the Litany of Our Lady of Montligeon on behalf of the holy souls. (This is in *The Rosary for the Holy Souls in Purgatory*.)
- Join the Association of the Holy Souls in Fátima. Write to: Dominican Nuns of the Perpetual Rosary, Pius XII Monastery, Rua do Rosario 1, 2495 Fátima, Portugal.
- Start a First Friday vigil at your parish.
- Join a parish bereavement committee.
- Start a purgatorial society in your parish.

SUMMER DEVOTIONS AND SPIRITUAL PRACTICES (JULY/AUGUST/SEPTEMBER)

- Practice the ancient tradition of praying the Stations of the Cross for the holy souls for thirty-three days at home or at church and, if possible, going to Mass on each of those days in honor of Our Lord's thirty-three years on earth. Many favors have been obtained by this means. (See *The Way of the Cross for the Holy Souls in Purgatory*.)
- Recite the Precious Blood Litany during the month of July. The holy souls need the precious blood of Jesus. (See *Prayers for Eternal Life*.)

- Go on your own "purgatory pilgrimage" by visiting local parishes and designated shrines within your diocese. At each, pray for the holy souls. Visit the shrines of "purgatory saints," those who were especially devoted to the souls in purgatory.
- When passing a cemetery, pray the Eternal Rest Prayer.
- Take a "prayer stroll" through your local cemetery to pray for all those buried there. Bring holy water to sprinkle on the graves. (It is one of the first sacramentals of the Church. Holy water refreshes the holy souls.)
- Visit the graves of your loved ones and clean sites in a spirit of prayer and penance.
- Around the graves of your loved ones, plant flowers in their honor.
- Offer the Portiuncula Indulgence for the holy souls on August 2. (See in Part II: The Great Pardon: The Portiuncula Indulgence.)
- Pray the Novena to Our Lady of Knock from August 14 to August 22. (See Appendix: Novena Prayers and Additional Resources.)
- Pray the Novena to Our Lady of Sorrows from September 7 to September 15. (Check the Internet.)
- Pray the Novena to St. Nicholas of Tolentino prior to his feast day, from September 2 to September 10. (See Appendix: Novena Prayers and Additional Resources.)
- Pray the Novena Prayer to St. John Macias prior to his feast day, from September 10 to September 18. (See Appendix: Novena Prayers and Additional Resources.)
- Pray the Eternal Rest Prayer on your rosary beads.
- Pray the Seven Penitential Psalms (seven psalms that express sorrow for one's sins). (This is in *Praying in the Presence of Our Lord for the Holy Souls*.)

- Pray Pope Benedict XVI's nine-day novena of meditations and prayer for the holy souls. (See Appendix: Novena Prayers and Additional Resources.)

Fall Devotions and Spiritual Practices (October/November/December)

- An indulgence is granted the Christian faithful who devoutly visit a cemetery and pray, even if only mentally, for the dead. This indulgence is applicable only to the souls in purgatory. This indulgence is a *plenary* one from November 1 through November 8 and can be gained on each one of these days. On the other days of the year this indulgence is a *partial* one. (See in Part II: Be Greedy and Grab the Grace of Indulgences.)
- Double up on prayers and sacrifices for departed loved ones and friends during this powerful season of the dead. Don't waste your sufferings.
- Pray the Litany for the Faithful Departed. (This is in *Praying in the Presence of Our Lord for the Holy Souls*.)
- Pray the Office for the Dead.
- Pray the *Rosary for the Holy Souls in Purgatory* before the Blessed Sacrament.
- Enroll your family and friends, living and deceased, in spiritual memberships, a spiritual solidarity of prayer.
- Visit cemeteries with your children. Teach youth to pray the Eternal Rest Prayer. Again, sprinkle holy water on the graves in the cemetery.
- Pray the Litany to the Guardian Angels during the month of October. (This is in *Prayers for Eternal Life*.)
- Light blessed candles. The burning candle is a sign of our prayer, a bright, silent intercessor for the holy souls.
- Offer your Mass and indulgence for the holy souls on Christmas Day. Remember that any indulgences you give to the departed come back to you!

- Place a special ornament on your Christmas tree or wreath in remembrance of the holy souls.
- Share stories and pictures of deceased family members, remembering them in prayer.
- Go to weekly Eucharistic Adoration holy hours using *Praying in the Presence of Our Lord for the Holy Souls.* Adorers assume the office of mediators on behalf of the members of the Church Militant and the Church Suffering.
- Pray the *Thirty-Day Devotions for the Holy Souls.*
- Include the St. Gertrude prayer in your Christmas cards. (See in Part II: During the Month of Souls, Recall Gertrude the Great.)
- During the month of November celebrate "Cemetery Sundays" with your family, parish, or diocese. Visit the local and neighboring cemeteries and pray for all those buried there.
- Celebrate the Day of the Dead on November 2.
- Explore traditions of your heritage on how All Souls Day is celebrated. Pass them on.
- Pre-plan your funeral; arrange to have purgatory material distributed at your wake and funeral to encourage all to pray for you and the holy souls.

APPENDIX
Novena Prayers and Additional Resources

Purgatory Passages from the Old and New Testaments

2 Maccabees 12:39-45

Matthew 12:32; 18:32-35

Luke 7:47; 12:58; 16:19-31

1 Corinthians 3:10-15

2 Corinthians 5:10

Revelation 6: 9-11; 21:27

Cf. 1 Samuel 2:6, Psalm 56:13, Psalm 68:20, Isaiah 57:2, and Malachi 3:2-3

For complete purgatory passages and references, see my book *The Rosary for the Holy Souls in Purgatory.*

Eternal Rest Prayer

Eternal rest grant unto them, O Lord, and let perpetual light shine upon them. May their souls and all the souls of the faithful departed, through the mercy of God, rest in peace. Amen.

Novena to Our Lady of Knock

This novena may be made at home or in the local church. This gives you a share in the Masses and prayers being offered each day at the shrine during the national public novena:

In the name of the Father, and of the Son, and of the Holy Spirit. Amen.

Give praise to the Father Almighty,
to his Son, Jesus Christ the Lord,
to the Spirit who lives in our hearts,
both now and forever. Amen.

Our Lady of Knock, Queen of Ireland, you gave hope to your people in a time of distress, and comforted them in sorrow. You have inspired countless pilgrims to pray with confidence to your divine Son, remembering his promise, "Ask and you shall receive, seek and you shall find."

Help me to remember that we are all pilgrims on the road to heaven. Fill me with love and concern for my brothers and sisters in Christ, especially those who live with me. Comfort me when I am sick, lonely or depressed. Teach me how to take part ever more reverently in the Holy Mass. Give me a greater love of Jesus in the Blessed Sacrament. Pray for me now, and at the hour of my death. Amen.

Lamb of God, you take away the sins of the world,

Have mercy on us.

Lamb of God, you take away the sins of the world;

Have mercy on us.

Lamb of God, you take away the sins of the world;

Grant us peace.

St. Joseph:
Chosen by God to be
the Husband of Mary,
the Protector of the Holy Family,
the Guardian of the Church.
Protect all families in their work and recreation
and guard us on our journey through life.

(Repeat the Lamb of God, etc.)

St. John:

> Beloved Disciple of the Lord,
> faithful priest,
> teacher of the Word of God.
> Help us to hunger for the Word,
> to be loyal to the Mass
> and to love one another.

(Repeat the Lamb of God, etc.)

Our Lady of Knock,	**Pray for us.**
Refuge of Sinners,	**Pray for us.**
Queen assumed into Heaven,	**Pray for us.**
Queen of the Rosary,	**Pray for us.**
Mother of Nazareth,	**Pray for us.**
Queen of Virgins,	**Pray for us.**
Health of the Sick,	**Pray for us.**
Our Lady and Mother,	**Pray for us.**
Our Lady, Mother of the Church,	**Pray for us.**

(Here mention your own special intentions.)

With the Angels and Saints, let us pray:

> Give praise to the Father Almighty,
> to his Son, Jesus Christ the Lord,
> to the Spirit who lives in our hearts,
> both now and forever. Amen.

(The Rosary or Mass and Holy Communion are recommended each day.)

Prayer to Our Lady of Montligeon

Our Lady, deliverer of all mankind,
have mercy on all our dearly departed,
especially those who are most
in need of the Lord's mercy.

Intercede for those who have passed away
so that the purifying love of God
may lead them to full deliverance.

May our prayers, united with the prayers
of the whole Church,
obtain for them a joy beyond all expectations,
and bring consolation and relief
to our friends in sorrow and distress
here on earth.

Mother of the Church,
on our journey towards life everlasting,
as pilgrims here on earth,
help us to live better lives each day.

Heal the wounds of our hearts and souls.
Help us to become witnesses of the Invisible,
to already seek that which the eye cannot see.
Make us apostles of Hope,
like watchmen awaiting the dawn.

Refuge of Sinners and Queen of All Saints,
gather us all together one day in the Father's House,
for the eternal resurrection,
through Jesus Christ our Lord.
Amen.

Novena Prayer to Blessed Mary of Providence

Blessed Mary of Providence, you gave praise and thanks to God through your love and care not only of the living but also toward those who have gone before us. Help me to grow in this way of life. Take my needs and desires today *(name your intentions)* and hear the prayers of those who call upon you. Help us in our endeavors to carry out our resolutions, to lead a prayerful life, to die a good death, and be with one another in eternal happiness. Amen.

Novena Prayer to St. John Macias

We come to you, Holy Brother John, for we know well the power of your intercession in the heavenly courts. Increase in us true sorrow for sin, fidelity to the Christian Gospel of love, and total resignation to the will of God in all things. Humbly we beg you to intercede for us that our petitions be granted, if they be in accord with the divine will. We ask this through Christ our Lord. Amen.

(Pray a decade of the Rosary for your intentions.)

Septenarium Prayers of St. Nicholas of Tolentino

A devotion of seven consecutive days of Masses offered or, where this is not possible, seven Holy Communions accompanied by these prayers and reflections for the holy souls in purgatory. These prayers contain certain instances of St. Nicholas' life along with the places of occurrence. We can only faintly imagine the glory we give to God and the assistance rendered to our "friends" the holy souls.

First Day

Our Father, Hail Mary, Glory Be.
St. Nicholas, patron of the holy souls, pray for us.

Prayer

O good Jesus, you mystically die upon our altars, thus renewing the oblation of Calvary for our sakes. We kneel now in silence before your tabernacle, as Mary Magdalene and John and your Blessed Mother knelt in the silence of that awful moment when the angel of death spread his wings around the cross.

As our thoughts follow you down from Calvary to that mysterious region where the immense multitude of souls who died before you long awaited your redemption, so now, dear Jesus, we plead for the release of the souls detained in that other state — the exile of purgatory. We plead through the prayers of the angels that serve you, through the merits of the saints who surround you, through the merits of the Saint of Tolentino, the memory and efficacy of whose great charity towards the holy souls is our encouragement to approach your divine bounty.

In your compassion for these souls, deign once again, through the intercession of St. Nicholas, to open the gates of purgatory that heaven may see the passing of multitudes to eternal happiness.

Glory Be.

Eternal rest grant unto them, O Lord, and let perpetual light shine upon them. May their souls and all the souls of the faithful departed, through the mercy of God, rest in peace. Amen.

Concluding Prayer

Grant we beseech you, O Almighty God, that your Church, illumined with the glory of the prodigies and miracles of St. Nicholas, your blessed confessor, may by his merits and intercession enjoy perpetual unity and peace, through Christ our Lord. Amen.

Second Day

Our Father, Hail Mary, Glory Be.

St. Nicholas, patron of the holy souls, pray for us.

Prayer

Remember, O gentle and compassionate Lord, the pity that stirred your heart when the cry of misery and sorrow came to your ears in Israel; how your eyes searched the rocks for the poor lepers who called out to you; how you reached out your hand to the child of Jairus, and to the widow's son of Naim; how the tears came to your eyes at the tomb of Lazarus.

Look now upon the region of suffering where souls that love you await the touch of your mercy. Through the merits of your own sufferings which appeased the eternal justice, extend your hand once more in its infinite power to relieve the holy souls in their sufferings.

O Lord, hear our prayers, unworthy though they be. We unite them with the prayers of your servant St. Nicholas, with the prayers of his childhood in the grotto of Sant' Angelo, with the prayers which he offered you for the holy souls through the silent hours of the night, with the prayers in which he blessed your infinite goodness and mercy for your miraculous aid in his ministry. Hear our prayers for the souls in purgatory and grant them eternal rest.

As on first day:

Glory Be.

Eternal Rest.

Concluding Prayer.

Third Day

Our Father, Hail Mary, Glory Be.

St. Nicholas, patron of the holy souls, pray for us.

Prayer

Remember, O divine and merciful Lord, your compassion for the soul of Gentile Judiani, for whom St. Nicholas besought mercy. You gave that dying man the grace of repentance; you suspended the rigor of your justice; and accepting the merits and suffrages of St. Nicholas on his behalf, you remitted the punishment deserved by his sins.

Show now, O Lord, the same gentle pity to the penitent souls in purgatory who in human frailty offended your majesty and holiness. Listen to the prayer of your saint to which we in our lowliness unite our supplications and grant the holy souls relief from their sufferings, so that with the blessed in heaven they may join their voices in praise of your mercy.

As on first day:
    Glory Be.
    Eternal Rest.
    Concluding Prayer.

Fourth Day

Our Father, Hail Mary, Glory Be.
St. Nicholas, patron of the holy souls, pray for us.

Prayer

O ever blessed and adorable God, we remember how you permitted your servant St. Nicholas to see a multitude of poor sufferers expiating their sins in purgatory. How the vision overwhelmed him with grief and his heart poured out its gratitude to you when you accepted the penances and prayers which he offered you in union with the infinite merits of the Holy Sacrifice.

On the seventh day of his continued appeal to your mercy you opened wide the gates of purgatory and paradise and permitted his eyes to see the great multitudes that were passing to their eternal rest with you. Hasten now, O Lord, to show the wonders of your mercy. Grant through the devotion of the septenarium of the saint that many of the faithful departed may pass this day from darkness and suffering to the light of the beatific vision.

As on first day:
> Glory Be.
> Eternal Rest.
> Concluding Prayer.

Fifth Day

Our Father, Hail Mary, Glory Be.
St. Nicholas, patron of the holy souls, pray for us.

Prayer

O ever bountiful and merciful Lord, you have glorified the memory of the Saint of Tolentino by countless and extraordinary miracles, giving to his prayers a wondrous efficacy and to his hand an astonishing healing power; through you he solaced and healed the afflicted; through you he restored the dead child to its mother's embrace; to your pitying mercy he led the despairing and the penitent. Through the holiness and merits of your saint, may the holy souls be admitted to your mercies and to the embrace of your compassionate love. Grant them the solace of your clemency and eternal happiness with your saints.

As on first day:
> Glory Be.
> Eternal Rest.
> Concluding Prayer.

Sixth Day

Our Father, Hail Mary, Glory Be.
St. Nicholas, patron of the holy souls, pray for us.

Prayer

Remember, O Lord, the cry of the poor victim on the lonely Italian mountain. That cry which found no pity in cruel human hearts found pity in heaven because it invoked your all-holy name and the venerated name of the saint of Tolentino.

The death of sin and that poor soul became no obstacle to your mercy. O good Jesus, how wonderful are your ways in dealing with human souls! A boundless ocean of merits and mercy surrounds your Calvary and the cross upon which you were immolated by cruel hands. Behold, we turn our eyes to you upon the cross and upon the altar, and our hearts overflow with confidence. In that confidence we appeal to you for mercy for our own unworthy souls and for the souls of all the faithful departed. Let your own merits make amends for their failings, and take them to your heart in the land of eternal happiness.

As on first day:
> Glory Be.
> Eternal Rest.
> Concluding Prayer.

Seventh Day

Our Father, Hail Mary, Glory Be.
St. Nicholas, patron of the holy souls, pray for us.

Prayer

O Blessed Mother of our Redeemer, remember that dark hour beneath the cross when the dying lips of Jesus consecrated us to your mother-love and through the tender compassion which he kindled in your heart at that moment, bear to the eternal throne the supplications which we offer for your children in purgatory.

In humility, we lift our eyes to your divine Son. We see him through the light of faith in the Holy Sacrifice of the Mass or abiding in the hallowed shelter of the tabernacle, and we remember, dear Mother, that your own pure heart was the first altar close to which he reposed here on earth. Would that we could bring into his presence a faith and a love like yours!

Help us, dear Mother; supplement our weak efforts; give your powerful aid to our prayers for the souls in purgatory. Through the infinite merits of the cross, through your tender compassion for the souls of all your children, through your love and the love of St. Nicholas for Jesus present in the adorable sacrament of the altar, we plead for the release of the souls in purgatory.

As on first day:
  Glory Be.
  Eternal Rest.
  Concluding Prayer.

A Novena of Meditations and Prayers with Pope Benedict XVI

Throughout his pontificate, Pope Benedict XVI has spoken on the holy souls and the need to remember them. The following are excerpts from his homilies, encyclicals, and addresses to offer us prayerful meditations and insight. Let yourself be enlightened in mind and heart.

After each section, recite an Our Father, Hail Mary, and Glory Be for the holy souls in purgatory.

Day One
The sacrament of baptism marks us for entry into the Communion of Saints

At the end of life, death deprives us of all that is earthly, but not of that Grace and that sacramental "character" by virtue of which we are indissolubly associated with our Lord and Savior's Paschal Mystery. Emptied of all but clothed in Christ: thus do the baptized cross the threshold of death and are presented to the just and merciful God.

In order, that the white garment received in Baptism may be purified of every speck and every stain, the Community of believers offers the Eucharistic Sacrifice and other prayers of suffrage for those whom death has called to pass from time to eternity.

Praying for the dead is a noble practice that implies belief in the resurrection of the dead, in accordance with what has been revealed to us by Sacred Scripture and, in a complete way, by the Gospel. (Homily, November 4, 2006)

Day Two
An invitation to trust in God

It is consoling and salutary, in praying for the deceased, to meditate upon Jesus' trust in his Father and thus let oneself be enveloped by the serene light of this absolute abandonment of the Son to the will of his *"Abba."* Jesus knows that the Father is always with him (cf. Jn 8:29); that together they are one (cf. 10:30).

He knows that his own death must be a "baptism," in other words, an "immersion" into God's love (cf. Lk 12:50), and he goes to meet it, certain that the Father will bring about in him the ancient prophecy. "After two days he will revive us; on the third day he will raise us up, that we may live before him" (Hos 6:2). (Homily, November 5, 2007)

Day Three
My souls thirsts for God, for the living God

"When shall I come and behold the face of God?" (Ps 42[41]:1-3). This thirst contains a truth that does not betray, a hope that does not disappoint. It is a thirst which even in the darkest night lights the way towards the source of life.

"Why are you cast down, O my soul, and why are you disquieted within me? Hope in God, for I shall again praise him, the salvation of my face and my God" (cf. vv.5-6). "Let not your hearts be troubled; believe in God, believe also in me. In my Father's house are many rooms."

These words reveal all their marvelous truth; not even death can make the believer's hope fruitless, because for our sake Christ entered the sanctuary of heaven, and it is there that he desires to lead us, having prepared a place for us (cf. Jn 14:1-3). With God there is room for all. (Homily, November 5, 2007)

Day Four
God is the true wisdom that never ages

Venerable old age is not only length of years, but wisdom and a pure existence, without malice. If the Lord prematurely calls the righteous to himself, it is due to a loving design for him that is unknown to us. The premature death of a person dear to us becomes an invitation not to persist in living in a mediocre way, but to strain towards the fullness of life.

The world considers a long life fortunate, but God, more than age, looks at the uprightness of heart. The world gives credit to the "wise" and "intelligent," while God prefers the "lowly." The general teaching we can draw from this is that there are two dimensions to reality. In reality, true life, eternal life already begins in this world, although within the precariousness of human history; eternal life begins in the measure to which we open ourselves to the mystery of God and welcome it in our midst.

It is God, the Lord of life, in whom "we live and move and have our being." (Acts 17:28.) (Homily, November 3, 2008)

Day Five
"I shall dwell in the house of the LORD forever" (Ps 23:6)

Even if they [the deceased souls] must expiate their part of the punishment due to the human frailty that marks all of us, helping us to stay humble, fidelity to Christ permits them to enter into the freedom of the children of God.

If, however, having to part with them saddened us, faith fills us with an intimate comfort at the thought that, as it has been for the Lord Jesus, and always thanks to him, death no longer has power over them (cf. Rom 6:9). (Homily, November 3, 2008)

Day Six
The Church's prayer of suffrage relies on the prayer of Jesus

"Father, I desire that they also, whom you have given me, may be with me where I am, to behold my glory" (Jn 17:24).

We intend our prayers of suffrage to be united with this prayer of the Lord which is priestly *par excellence*. Christ substantiated his entreaty to the Father with the gift of himself on the Cross; let us offer our prayers in union with the Eucharistic Sacrifice, which is the real and actual representation of that unique and saving self-emptying. (Homily, November 4, 2006)

Day Seven
"We should be holy and blameless before him" (Eph 1:4)

Our prayer of praise to God and veneration of the blessed spirits which today's liturgy presents to us as "a great multitude which no man could number, from every nation, from all tribes and peoples and tongues" (Rev 7:9), is united with prayers of suffrage for all who have preceded us in passing from this world to eternal life.

To tell the truth, the Church invites us to pray for them every day, also offering our daily sufferings and efforts so that, completely purified, they may be admitted to the eternal joy of light and peace in the Lord. (Angelus, November 1, 2007)

Day Eight
Practicing Christian hope

The souls of the departed can receive "solace and refreshment" through the Eucharist, prayer and almsgiving.

The belief that love can reach into the afterlife, that reciprocal giving and receiving is possible, in which our affection for one another continues beyond the limits of death — this has been a fundamental conviction of Christianity throughout the ages and it remains a source of comfort today.

Who would not feel the need to convey to their departed loved ones a sign of kindness, a gesture of gratitude or even a request for pardon? Our hope is always essentially also hope for others; only thus is it truly hope for me, too. (*Spe Salvi*, November 30, 2007)

Day Nine
Their names are written in heaven

Let us unite our common prayer and raise it to the Father of all goodness and mercy so that, through the intercession of Mary Most Holy, the encounter with the fire of his love quickly purifies our late departed friends from every imperfection and transforms them to the praise of his glory. And we pray, that we, pilgrims on the earth, will always keep our eyes and heart focused on the ultimate goal for which we yearn, the House of the Father. So be it! (Homily, November 3, 2008)

Final Prayer

The Virgin Mary is resplendent at the center of the Assembly of Saints, "created beings all in lowliness surpassing, as in height, above them all" (Dante, *Paradise*, Canto XXXIII, 2).

By putting our hand in hers, we feel encouraged to walk more enthusiastically on the path of holiness. Let us entrust to her our daily work and pray to her today for our dear departed, in the intimate hope of meeting one another all together one day in the glorious Communion of Saints.

Amen.

BIBLIOGRAPHY

Alberione, Very Rev. James, S.S.P., S.T.D. *Lest We Forget.* Boston, MA: Daughters of St. Paul, 1967.

Alighieri, Dante. *Divine Comedy.* Translated by Dorothy L. Sayers. New York: Penguin Books, 1955.

Biver, Comte Paul, *Père Lamy.* Rockford, IL: TAN Publishers, 1973.

Bonaventure, St. *The Soul's Journey Into God, The Tree of Life, The Life of St. Francis.* Translation by Ewert Cousins. Mahwah, NJ: Paulist Press, 1978.

A Calendar of Indulgences. Peoria, IL: Bridegroom Press, 2009.

Catherine of Genoa. *Purgation and Purgatory: The Spiritual Dialogue.* Mahwah, NJ: Paulist Press, 1979.

Congregation of Marians. *Diary of Saint Maria Faustina Kowalska.* Stockbridge, MA: Marian Press, 1987.

"Dialogues of Pope St. Gregory" in *The Fathers of the Church.* New York: Fathers of the Church, Inc., 1959.

Dostoyevsky, Fyodor, *The Brothers Karamazov.* Translation by Constance Garnett. Kansas City, MO: The Lowell Press, 1912.

Garside, Rev. Charles B., M.A. *The Helpers of the Holy Souls.* New York: The Helpers of the Holy Souls, 1898.

Giuli, Giuseppe, O.S.A. *Saint Nicholas of Tolentine.* Tolentine, Italy: Basilica and Sanctuary of Saint Nicholas, 1999.

Good, Eileen. *Places Apart-Lough Derg.* Dublin, Ireland: Veritas Publications, 2003.

Hampsch, John H., C.M.F. *Healing Your Family Tree.* Santa Barbara, CA: Queenship Publishing, 1989.

The Handbook of Indulgences, Norms, and Grants. New York: Catholic Book Publishing Co., 1991.

Huguet, Jean Joseph. *Consoling Thoughts of St. Francis de Sales.* New York: Fr. Pustet & Co., 1958.

Jugie, Father Martin. *Purgatory.* Westminster, MD: The Newman Press, 1949.

Lasance, Rev. F.X. *Holy Souls Book.* New York: Benziger Brothers, 1922.

The Life and Revelations of St. Gertrude the Great. Rockford, IL: TAN Publishers, 2002.

Lucia, Sister. *Calls from the Message of Fatima.* Still River, MA: The Ravengate Press, 2000.

Nageleisen, Rev. John A. *Charity for the Suffering Souls.* Rockford, IL: TAN Publishers, 1994.

Parente, Father Allesio, O.F.M. Cap. *The Holy Souls "Viva Padre Pio."* Foggia, Italy: Our Lady of Grace Capuchin Friary, 1994.

Ratzinger, Joseph Cardinal. *God and the World: Believing and Living in Our Time.* San Francisco: Ignatius Press, 2002.

———. *The Ratzinger Report: An Exclusive Interview on the State of the Church.* San Francisco: Ignatius Press, 1985.

Rogalewski, Rev. Tadeusz, MIC. *Founder of the Marians.* Stockbridge, MA: Marians of the Immaculate Conception, 1997.

Sadlier, Mrs. J. *Purgatory.* New York: D. & J. Sadlier & Company, 1886.

Schmöger, C.SS.R., Very Rev. Carl, *The Life of Anne Catherine Emmerich*, Vol. 1. Rockford, IL: TAN Publishers, 1976.

Windeatt, Mary Fabyan. *Saint John Masias* [Macias]. New York: Sheed and Ward, 1944; Rockford, IL: TAN Publishers, 1972.

INDEX

135

ABOUT THE COVER

Praying with the Saints for the Holy Souls in Purgatory is one of the most efficacious ways of helping the holy souls to be released from their great suffering.

The cover presents a "behind the veil" glimpse of the constant intercession of the saints for the holy souls. These great saints — who, while on earth, were devoted to the holy souls — have now earned a special place of intercession before the Throne of Mercy in heaven. Now, as they hear our prayers rising to them for the holy souls, they in turn plead to the Mother of Mercy, whose "little children" are undergoing intense suffering and purification below. Because they are her children, she intercedes for them to her Infant Son. The Infant Jesus, who cannot deny His Mother, holds out the Crown of Life to all.

The composition is designed in the tradition of two different balances that provide motion, and conformity, to the overall appearance: in heaven, *symmetrical balance, or perfect balance,* is used to symbolize peace and the perfect order of heaven while, below in purgatory, *asymmetrical balance* is used to create a balanced composition but with the balance slightly offset, symbolizing perfection in the making. Overall, the postures, gestures, and flowing robes create a delightful rhythm of flowing, suggesting a perpetual motion that moves the eye.

At the top left, SS. Padre Pio and Nicholas of Tolentino plead for the holy souls. Padre Pio wears the gloves he wore on earth to conceal the stigmata, but now they are an honor of glory. Below them, Pope St. Gregory the Great intercedes for the soul of a young woman who, through the thirty-day Gregorian Masses, can feel the soothing effects of prayer as she instinctively reaches up to Gregory, who reaches out to her. To the right, above, St. Catherine of Genoa, who has been reading her *Treatise on Purgatory* to the Infant Jesus, pauses so that she can look down from heaven and see the wonderful results of her prayers: an angel freeing the soul on behalf of whom she was asked to intercede. Behind her is St. Gertrude the Great praying for the perfection and release of the holy souls. Above her are the golden vaults of heaven encrusted with the pearls that the Lord showed her that were the prayers for the holy souls. Pearls are a symbol of perfection through purification, as they start with something unclean, such as silt or a grain of sand caught in a mollusk, and through much time and suffering the mollusk forms a beautiful, shining, iridescent pearl. Gertrude was also given a vision of how the holy souls appear as sparks of light as they are released from purgatory and ascend to heaven. These brilliant sparks adorn the celestial firmament in the form of eight-point stars representing the New Day, which was created by the Resurrection.

On the right side of the scene, Blessed Mary of Providence looks out directly at the viewer, pointing to the title of the book so as to encourage all to come learn of the wonderful efficacious ways of *Praying with the Saints for the Holy Souls in Purgatory*. The title then draws us into the book, which for us, the Church Militant, becomes a "place" where we are incorporated into the Communion of Saints, as we learn from these great saints how to pray for the holy souls.

Original Art Features

- Raised and burnished 23kt Gold
- 23kt Powder Gold
- Genuine Ultramarine Blue from Lapis Lazuli
- Malachite
- Vermilion

- Iragazine Red
- Red Jasper
- Lead White
- Titanium White
- Chinese White
- Sepia from the Adriatic Cuttlefish
- Ocher from the Island of Elba
- Caput Mortuum
- Naples Yellow
- Other dry ground pigments on Wyndstone Parchment
- Actual art: 7.5 inches by 11.25 inches

JED GIBBONS
Illustrator

ABOUT THE AUTHOR

Susan Tassone has long been a passionate champion for the holy souls in purgatory and is recognized as leading the "purgatory movement" in the United States. She is a best-selling author whose first work, *The Way of the Cross for the Holy Souls in Purgatory*, has sold more than 70,000 copies. (See the next page for a complete listing of Susan's books.) In addition to her many writings on behalf of those in purgatory, she is a popular speaker and frequent guest on radio and television shows.

Susan holds a master's degree in religious education from Loyola University and is a consultant for a major non-profit philanthropic organization. She had the honor and privilege of being granted two private audiences with Pope John Paul II, who bestowed a special blessing upon her and her ministry for the holy souls.

Visit Susan Tassone's website at: *www.susantassone.com*.